WHAT PEOPLE ARE SAYING ABOUT
AN ENTREPRENEUR IS FOR ALL SEASONS

Dr. Bruce Douglas credits his own mentors as foundational to his success in work and life. In turn, Bruce has mentored hundreds of people during his career. He has dedicated much of his time over the years to education, working to improve the systems and expand access. Now, he has written a powerful book that shares with a broader audience the wisdom and insight that can only come from decades of proven experience.

An Entrepreneur for All Seasons candidly describes Bruce's successes and failures, highlighting the skills and principles for success in academe, politics and social endeavors as well as in the office and boardroom. His commitment to lifelong learning is reflected throughout the book and he adeptly illustrates education, from grade school to graduate school, as key to opportunity.

Weaving personal experiences and anecdotal stories with practical advice and lessons learned from a diverse career, Bruce offers a unique perspective on entrepreneurship. Readers will develop a better understanding of how entrepreneurship has the power to do much more than just create successful businesses; it can transform the world around them. They will have new insights into how they, too, can become an Entrepreneur for All Seasons.

— Jeb Bush,
former Florida Governor

"I'm forever grateful to Mr. Douglas and his wife for their passion to affect positive change. Their efforts and commitment to education and philanthropy were an important part in my development from an early age. Whenever someone asks "What is your life story?" I always include Mr. and Mrs. Douglas as contributing factors to my success and the man I have become. An Entrepreneur for ALL Seasons shares many of the important lessons Mr. Douglas instilled in me during my youth. This book is a wonderful source of inspiration and a great resource for achieving success."

— Jermain L. Pettis,
Vice President, Commercial Banking

"This book is full of anecdotal stories and quips from an entrepreneurial life that has impacted many in the corporate sector as well as the non-profit and higher education fields. Through each story, the reader is able to hear the voice of wisdom speak honestly regarding battles won and battles lost. Many, who know Bruce well, will recognize this voice as the authors' as his mannerisms, intonation and communicative traits jump off the pages in written form. Much can be learned from a man who has shown resolve through many challenging personal and professional circumstances."

— **Scott Rich,** President,
Sterling College

"Bruce says we are to be an entrepreneur with our whole life, not just in our business. In this personal and informative book, he gives concrete examples of how he has done this throughout his career. Reading this book will inspire you to be an entrepreneur in every season of your life."

— **James M. Seneff, Jr.,** Executive Chairman,
CNL Financial Group

"Bruce Douglas has written an engaging and valuable book that is a "must read" for all ambitious leaders in business, politics, and education. He provides lessons in entrepreneurial leadership that he extracts from his own experiences about which he is brutally honest. Douglas provides helpful advice on the value of failure, the importance of integrity, and the benefits of persistence and good humor. I recommend the book unreservedly.

— **Rita Bornstein, Ph.D.,**
President Emerita & Cornell Professor
of Philanthropy and Leadership Development, *Rollins College*

"In his new book, An Entrepreneur Is for All Seasons, *Dr. Bruce Douglas offers readers an eminently readable analysis of the habits and traits of an entrepreneur. A successful serial entrepreneur himself, Dr. Douglas develops and illustrates principles by frequent and excellent use of anecdotes from a business and professional career that has spanned seven decades. Remarkably, he has had successful experience as an officer in the U. S. Navy, a civil and construction engineer, the owner of a thriving construction and development company, a university trustee, and a transformative president of a small, church-related liberal arts college.*

Through this rich lifetime of service, Dr. Douglas has applied an entrepreneur's focus, energy, ability to recognize and manage risk, openness to new ideas and experiences, and desire to make a positive difference in both his personal and professional life. A man of faith and integrity, he offers readers a model for thoughtful, energetic action to identify and solve problems. This reader was particularly impressed by his habit of viewing the client's or customer's interests as paramount. In doing so, he created what we might characterize as de facto partnerships that became the basis of enduring and profitable relationships. Dr. Douglas has given us a fascinating book filled with lessons for a productive lifetime."

— **Dr. John C. Hitt,** President,
University of Central Florida

"… an extremely interesting read. By walking through a life of entrepreneurship, Bruce provides the reader with wisdom and inspiration. His failures and successes provide potential entrepreneurs with priceless insights and guidance. Woven through the book are important thoughts on communication, listening and leadership. This is a book I could not put down. In full disclosure, I have known and worked with Bruce for over 15 years, and was intrigued with the insights and experiences that formed a lifetime of entrepreneurship and responsible leadership to his companies, communities and his faith. This is a must read for anyone who thinks they may want to be an entrepreneur."

— **Dr. Craig M. McAllaster,** Acting President,
Rollins College

"It was an easy read that provided the most important tools an entrepreneur would need to hit the ground running with a positive, confident outlook. If the entrepreneur is serious about success, and follows Bruce's leadership, he or she is guaranteed a future of continual success. I highly recommend this book as a "Must Read" for every entrepreneur starting a new company. We certainly will incorporate the book as a "Must Read" in our business.

— **Larry Walker,** Founding Partner,
NewGate Capital Partners

"I simply could not put this book down. I began reading, expecting a wise book on entrepreneurship, what I got was so much more. Bruce Douglas has crafted a memoir, chocked full of invaluable insights and lessons of an entrepreneurial life well lived. Everyone, from all walks and stages of life, can benefit from his wisdom."

— **Cari Coats, President,** C2 Advisors and Executive-in-Residence, *Rollins College Center for Advanced Entrepreneurship*

"The story of a life is often illustrative of the deepest values of a culture or person. Such is the case with the story of Bruce Douglas' life. It inspires, lifts up and defines a pathway. This book is a 'must read.'"

— **Lloyd A. Jacobs,** M.D., President Emeritus, *The University of Toledo*

"Dr. Douglas' life has been nothing short of remarkable -- and he's not done! This was a book that needed to be written. My biggest take-away was the importance of balancing the confidence you must have to effectively get things done with the humility to understand when you are wrong. As a man with his level of success, it would have been easy to ignore the sentiments of students and other faculty members of Sterling College, but Dr. Douglas was wise enough to understand that management, while ultimately in the direct hands of the leader, isn't complete without the input of those in the trenches."

— **Brett Andrews,** Partner, *NewGate Capital Partners*

"...a great book for the innovative leader, depicting essential entrepreneurial skills in action in all areas of life that one experiences...An amazing life story that depicts the success of an entrepreneurial leader in all areas of life he chose to pursue."

— **Tom McEvoy,** Interim Dean, *Rollins College Crummer Graduate School of Business*

"I have always associated Entrepreneurship with individuals interested only in starting their own businesses. But it's evident through Douglas' life that entrepreneurs are much more. Just as Douglas has done, entrepreneurs seek to leave contributions and stimulate change through their goals. It's evident that cultivating change is not accomplished overnight but instead requires hard work, determination, and high character with little room for others opinions. With Douglas' lustrous and diversified career he has proven

an individual can make a difference in several different arenas of life such as business, education, and politics. Reading Douglas' unique story and wisdom is encouraging for a young individual like me. I can personally relate to the apathetic and often times absent father Douglas mentions. It gives me hope and appreciation knowing there are other individuals who have succeeded before me despite direct support from family members."

— Jeremy D. Edwards, Associate,
NewGate Capital Partners

"I really enjoyed this book. It is well written and an easy read. I have been struggling with the idea that soon I won't be a student anymore and will have to be in the real world. This book honestly helped with my anxiety of starting over. Reading about Dr. Douglas's many "fresh starts" has calmed those thoughts of whether I can really do this and given me confidence for what is to come. The stories of other self-starters and their perseverance through rejection and other challenges were great and encouraging. I could definitely see recommending this to other seniors in my major (international business) or to any students in the new Entrepreneur major at Rollins.

One of my favorite parts was Dr. Douglas's description of the word entrepreneur.: "…defining the word entrepreneur purely in a business sense was too limiting. I prefer to think of it in much broader terms: as a method of approaching everything."

— Rebekah Benfield,
Graduating College Student

An
Entrepreneur
is for ALL
Seasons

*A complete guide for using entrepreneurship to
grow and succeed in all areas of your life.*

DR. BRUCE DOUGLAS

Published by Advantage, Charleston, South Carolina.
Member of Advantage Media Group.

ADVANTAGE is a registered trademark and the Advantage colophon is a trademark of Advantage Media Group, Inc.

Printed in the United States of America.

ISBN: 978-159932-554-5
LCCN: 2015931482

This publication is designed to provide accurate and authoritative information in regard to the subject matter covered. It is sold with the understanding that the publisher is not engaged in rendering legal, accounting, or other professional services. If legal advice or other expert assistance is required, the services of a competent professional person should be sought.

Advantage Media Group is proud to be a part of the Tree Neutral® program. Tree Neutral offsets the number of trees consumed in the production and printing of this book by taking proactive steps such as planting trees in direct proportion to the number of trees used to print books. To learn more about Tree Neutral, please visit www.treeneutral.com. To learn more about Advantage's commitment to being a responsible steward of the environment, please visit www.advantagefamily.com/green

Advantage Media Group is a publisher of business, self-improvement, and professional development books and online learning. We help entrepreneurs, business leaders, and professionals share their Stories, Passion, and Knowledge to help others Learn & Grow. Do you have a manuscript or book idea that you would like us to consider for publishing? Please visit advantagefamily.com or call 1.866.775.1696.

DEDICATION

This book is dedicated to Kathleen Cosgrove Douglas, my mother, who was always there to give insights and support. She focused on the better angels of our nature and the need to excel in every area of life. To paraphrase Lincoln, everything I am or ever hope to be I owe to my mother. Her insights echoed the Monday's Child poem, as I was at the cusp of Friday and Saturday; "Friday's child is loving and giving, Saturday's child works hard for a living."

ACKNOWLEDGEMENTS

Dean Baily, the preeminent developer in Northwestern Ohio, always challenged my thinking and enlarged my horizon.

Ren McPherson, CEO of the Dana Corporation, showed me the importance of people in your business, "In nine square feet around that machine in your factory, each person knows more about your endeavor than you do or ever will."

John Silber, President of Boston University, reviewed this entire book in its early stages over breakfast in a restaurant in Boston and made gigantic contributions to style and substance. He was my academic mentor as well.

Bill and Richard Gershenson, father and son, were mentors and friends in my business with their emphasis on relationships and a view of the bigger picture.

Jim Ruvolo, political leader and former chairman of the Ohio Democratic Party, showed a novice politician the ropes of political endeavors with unrelenting help and productive criticism.

Jim Fisher, the academic leader who made it possible for me to be a college president, with his insights and support at Sterling College.

Peter Kelly, lawyer and Democratic Party leader, showed me national and international trends and concepts that were crucial to my view of the nation and the world.

Dr. Rita Bornstein, Jeb Bush, Dr. John C. Hitt, J. Douglas Holladay, Dr. Lloyd A. Jacobs, Craig M. McAllaster, Tom McEvoy, Dr. Nagi Naganathan, Scott Rich, James M. Seneff, Jr., Cari Coats and Larry K. Walker, who were willing to read and to comment on the book at the galley proof stage, gave me insights and support in this endeavor, without which we would not have reached a publication date.

Wendy Kurtz, President of Elizabeth Charles & Associates, LLC, for her guidance as my publishing consultant, securing my publisher and managing the entire book process, from manuscript draft through final publication.

CONTENTS

"Trust thyself: Every heart vibrates to that iron string."

"To believe your own thought, to believe that what is true for you in your private heart is true for all men—that is genius . . . There is a time in every man's education when he arrives at the conviction that envy is ignorance; that imitation is suicide; that he must take himself for better, for worse, as his portion; that though the wide universe is full of good, no kernel of nourishing corn can come to him but through his toil bestowed on that plot of ground which is given to him to till."
—Ralph Waldo Emerson

FOREWORD

by

Dr. James L. Fisher

I first met Dr. Bruce Douglas through our common friend, Rear Admiral Richard Ridenour. Both had been involved as volunteers at Rollins College in Florida. I very much looked forward to meeting the remarkable entrepreneurial personality Dick described, who now wanted to become a college president. We met and, indeed, he was remarkable, a most extraordinary man: a very successful entrepreneur, community leader, mentor, philanthropist, gubernatorial candidate, university board chair, Navy veteran, and more.

After graduating with degrees in physics and engineering from Kalamazoo College and the University of Michigan (where he paid his way by working third shift at an automobile plant and numerous other jobs), and later a PhD in history from the University of Toledo and an MPA from Harvard, he chaired the board at the University of Toledo and later served as interim president. During this time, together with his good wife, Dee, among other things, he mentored and funded a group of African American middle school students through secondary school and college.

Now he wanted to become a college president. He and Dee, always good Catholics, found an interesting institution. He became president of Sterling College, a troubled Presbyterian liberal arts college in Kansas. In short, I had never known a more transformational presidency.

Beginning at a run, Bruce literally saved Sterling. (For four years we talked every Tuesday morning at seven.) Over the years, I had worked with more than 300 institutions and had never seen a college change so dramatically in such a short time. Bruce was a veritable whirling dervish (a classic hypomanic personality). He reorganized the administration, reduced costs, improved the curriculum, increased enrollment, improved faculty salaries (and he himself took no salary), raised funds, increased the endowment, and developed close relationships with the surrounding community and the state; indeed, a veritable renaissance.

Finally, I shamelessly admit that these memoirs moved me from admiration to fun to tears and back to admiration. Yes, it is the complete book on the fundamental importance of high goals, character, and hard work, but most of all character. Indeed, in my writing today, as I put pen to paper, I think: What would Bruce do? Dr. Bruce Douglas is the living embodiment of what I learned in the Marine Corps: The leader eats last.

James L. Fisher

INTRODUCTION

Who Becomes an Entrepreneur?

*"An entrepreneur is someone who will work
24 hours a day for themselves to avoid working
one hour a day for someone else."*
—Chris Guillebeau

STARTING A BUSINESS IS HARD.

S teve Jobs, who started Apple, Next, and Pixar, said it wasn't
for the mentally sane. You have to have a screw loose to want
to deal with all the conflict and pain. It exposes you to tremendous
uncertainty, produces profound anxiety, and places a great burden on
your most important relationships. All too often, the most successful
entrepreneurs have sacrificed marriages and friendships on the path
to success.

So why bother?

George Bernard Shaw might have been describing the entrepreneur when he wrote, "the people who get on in this world are the
people who get up and look for the circumstances they want, and, if
they can't find them, make them."

That is at the core of it: The desire to control your circumstances in order to make the most interesting life possible. Working for an employer may offer the feeling of security, but **entrepreneurship offers something quite different: an opportunity to transform your life and the lives of many around you**. In the words of Thomas Huxley, the biologist and close friend of Charles Darwin, "It is better for man to go wrong in freedom than to go right in chains." Such are the risks and rewards of the entrepreneurial life. When you lead as an entrepreneur and others catch your vision, it's marvelous. The feeling is of a crew with all members caring about each other and in sync. Rowers call it "swing."

During the three summers of my high school years, and a couple of summers when I was in college, I worked on the Pontiac Motor assembly line in Michigan, installing car dashboards. My pals and I were car freaks, and it was the late 1940s, a dramatic time in automobile production. New models appeared every September to great interest and acclaim. They were always fancier with bigger fins, more exciting features, and a rainbow of colors. Almost everyone in my high school class went to work in the plant after graduation.

But the truth was, for all the glamour surrounding cars, assembling them was meaningless, degrading work. The plant was filled with people with no aspirations or future plans. I found it difficult to concentrate because the work was so boring and the movement of the assembly line constant. We felt we were being treated like animals. There was no place to eat your lunch. There were no seats on the toilets. By working on the assembly line, I learned I didn't want to have that kind of career. That was not my goal in life.

That simple realization was one of the triggers for my life as an entrepreneur. Many people are quite happy being swept along by life's currents, drifting through school and college, turning up to work for 30 years and then retiring. But the entrepreneur wants something more: to understand the cause and effect of relationships and situations in his life and to take control of them to escape the factory floor and the tyranny of others.

Success in entrepreneurship isn't about getting to an IPO or appearing on the cover of a business magazine. It is about becoming the master of your own destiny and a problem solver for others. The world belongs to the problem solvers. Satisfaction in entrepreneurship comes when you know the world needs you.

When I think back over my own entrepreneurial life, what springs to mind are the moments of immense satisfaction arising from getting things done.

I remember being in Dayton, Ohio, while building three shopping centers. I came home on a Friday evening, tired and hungry. All I wanted was something to eat and a Scotch. But my wife told me that the board of trustees at the University of Toledo was staying in an emergency session until I arrived. The problem was a badly over-budget building project. The trustees needed me to help rescue the school's new arena, and as I got in the car, my exhaustion vanished. I realized there was no one more qualified than I to solve the problem. The university wanted me and the state needed me to come in and take control of the cost overruns. Winston Churchill said that there will be times in your life when someone taps you on the shoulder and says your special skills are needed to solve a problem. Be prepared.

I felt in that moment that all my years of building and running my construction business, the relationships I had made, the reputation I had built, and the knowledge I had gained had all been worth it.

I wanted to write this book to share my life's experiences in the same way that I do with the many young people I have mentored over the years. For six consecutive years, I gave the engineering leadership lecture at the University of Michigan Engineering School. After one of those talks, a small young man asked, "How can I make a lot of money like you have?"

I explained that the key was having mentors and reeled off all of the ones I'd had up to that point. There have been more since. Without mentors, enlightenment and feedback is limited.

This book is not a theoretical prescription for success but a series of lessons gleaned from experience. It is about applied entrepreneurship, if you like, in different settings, from business to academia to politics and my own life, and how an entrepreneurial attitude has shaped everything I've done.

Being an entrepreneur has provided me with great financial rewards, but much more importantly, it has given me meaningful friendships and a rich and interesting life.

SEEING OPPORTUNITY, NOT CHAOS

I believe entrepreneurship is at the heart of the free market system. With every technological leap, the speed at which businesses are created and destroyed increases. Entrepreneurs stand amidst this chaos and see opportunity rather than confusion. They never take the established order for granted but assume it will be smashed apart in their own lifetimes by newer, better ways of doing things. It is through entrepreneurs that industries, nations, and their economies renew themselves.

The recipe for entrepreneurial success is the source of much argument and academic inquiry. Some believe entrepreneurs are born with a set of innate traits and a genius for what they later do. In this view, entrepreneurs are fated by their genes to start businesses. Others give more credit to how entrepreneurs grow up and are acculturated.

In 2009, James Fisher and James Koch published a fascinating book, *Born, Not Made: The Entrepreneurial Personality*. They studied 230 chief executive officers, of whom 100 were founding CEOs and entrepreneurs, while the rest had been appointed to their jobs. Comparing the two groups, they concluded the entrepreneurs were different. For entrepreneurs, the status quo was always wrong and needed fixing.

According to Fisher and Koch, entrepreneurs are confident, decisive risk takers, willing to live at odds with the consensus. They may be charming and persuasive, but they use consensus and collegiality as a tool for achieving the changes they want. They are often psychologically removed from those around them, working "ahead of facts," as John Gartner, a psychologist at Johns Hopkins University put it, rather than "within facts." They don't acquire this kind of confidence over time; they are born with it. John Stewart Mill, a British philosopher, political economist, and civil servant, called it anticipating an idea that will become acceptable to future generations.

Fisher and Koch provided all kinds of examples in support of their thesis. They cited scientists who agreed that heredity influences everything from height, personality, intelligence, athletic ability, criminality, and, yes, sexual behavior. **The entrepreneurial personality means you are born with a predisposition toward risk taking.** Consider Walt Disney, who exhibited his taste for risk successfully playing poker as a soldier in World War I. That entrepreneurial spirit in Disney must be what allowed him to create two essentially phony cities in order to obtain complete control over the land and the development of the Walt Disney World complex. Or Fred Smith, the founder of Federal Express, who ignored the "C" he got at business school for his parcel-delivery concept and went ahead anyway. **Hostile circumstances and the disapproval of others are fuel rather than obstacles for the true entrepreneur.**

"Individuals who found their own firms view the world and its challenges differently than most others," wrote Fisher and Koch.

"They're more optimistic, extroverted, energetic, self-confident and visionary than the typical person and, critically, willing to take more risks. They'll often risk their personal financial fortunes and sometimes even their own lives in order to pursue their dreams. Entrepreneurship and risk-taking seem to be in their blood. Even though most entrepreneurs (perhaps 75 percent) eventually fail, they are seldom deterred. Like determined boxers who have taken an uppercut and been knocked to the canvas, many of them get back on their feet and come back for more. At a recent meeting of 10 entrepreneurs from the World President's Organization, the moderator asked everyone who had been through a bankruptcy to step forward. Thirty percent of the individuals did. Serial entrepreneurs, whether successful or not, often found new firms over and over again, or repeatedly developed new ventures and technologies."

Jim Clifton, CEO of Gallup, says the belief that anyone can be trained to be an entrepreneur is a mistaken assumption. His estimate is that for every thousand people there are only about three with the potential to develop an organization with $50 million or more in annual revenue.

While Fisher and Koch wrote that there was a significant genetic basis to the personality traits that matter most in successful entrepreneurs, success in entrepreneurship remains a matter of probabilities and tendencies. Some people might have all the right inherited traits but never succeed, while others might have few of them but thrive by focusing and developing those they do possess. Carrying this through generations is tough. The third generation Bruce Douglas is now in place at the Douglas Company, but the passion his father and grandfather share is latent. All of us, whatever traits we may have inherited, can work to be better entrepreneurs, but for those born lucky in this regard, that work will be easier, just as it is easier for a seven-foot center to dunk a basketball than it is for a five-foot-six point guard.

My genes trace to a minister grandfather who established a school in North Carolina and three churches in Michigan. My mother said the Biddle genes were in our makeup, and when I did my PhD dissertation on Nicholas Biddle, an uncle from nine generations back, the entrepreneurship heredity was clear: here was a man who established the Second National Bank of the United States and, in the process, cornered the cotton market in this country. When I did research at his desk in Andalusia, Pennsylvania looking at the Delaware River from his estate, it was as if he was standing at my shoulder as a mentor.

In his book *The Hypomanic Edge: The Link Between (A Little) Craziness and Success in America*, John Gartner wrote that hypomania is "a genetically based mild form of mania, [which] endows many of us with unusual energy, creativity, enthusiasm, and a propensity for taking risks. America has an extraordinarily high number of hypomanics—grandiose types who leap on every wacky idea that occurs to them, utterly convinced it will change the world. Market bubbles and ill-considered messianic crusades can be the downside. But there is an enormous upside in terms of spectacular entrepreneurial zeal, drive for innovation, and material success. Americans may have a lot of crazy ideas, but some of them lead to brilliant inventions."

The *Economist* describes the present time as another Cambrian moment, akin to the era 540 million years ago when life forms began to multiply and the animal kingdom became much more varied as more complex organisms could be assembled rapidly. Now is a time when the technologies of start-up production have become so evolved, cheap, and ubiquitous that they can be easily combined and recombined. **Launching entrepreneurial startups has become dirt cheap, which has radically changed their nature.**

Mark McCormack of IMG called it making connections that everyone else has almost thought of. Warren Benis, a widely published scholar on the subject of leadership, has asserted, "Leaders must encourage their organizations to dance to forms of music yet to be heard." The nature of entrepreneurs is to underestimate potential problems associated with their work as well as overestimate potential gains and profits. They are the modern equivalent of Voltaire's Dr. Pangloss (1759), who was constantly of the mind that conditions could not be better.

REBEL WITH A CAUSE

Entrepreneurs see internationalism and international trade as ecstatic activities—perceiving them as out of the ordinary, and for that reason attractive. Out of the ordinary experiences are things that most entrepreneurs instinctively crave. Emerson strongly suggested that if you enjoy stirring things up, frequently think outside the box, generate lots of innovative ideas, often violate the status quo, ignore the chain of command, and don't strongly believe in organizational structures, then you are much more likely to become an entrepreneur.

Hypomanics tend to be fast-talking multitaskers who barely sleep at night because their minds are constantly racing. They are in a near constant state of excitement that leads to frenzied production. Hypomanics like Sam Walton can be micromanagers, ceaselessly moving from task to task to escape boredom. Benjamin Franklin's obstreperous, independent-minded behavior suggests he was a hypomanic, as do Alexander Hamilton's frequent swings between depression and euphoria. I wonder if George Bernard Shaw didn't have the hypomanic in mind when he wrote in his essay on reasonableness: "The reasonable man adapts himself to the world; the unreasonable one persists in trying to adapt the world to himself. Therefore, all progress depends on the unreasonable man."

This collection of traits, Gartner argues, is genetic rather than learned, and is often found in entrepreneurs. It is not a series of traits that matches with classic definitions of happiness or contentment. The hypomanic is not inclined to sit under a tree and sip wine or ponder the gentle arc of a leaf falling from a branch. She may have bags under her eyes, a constantly jiggling knee, and a phone that never stops ringing. But in the midst of what looks to others like chaos and a recipe for exhaustion, the hypomanic finds purpose and satisfaction. Like Fisher and Koch, however, Gartner does not say that hypomania always leads to entrepreneurial success. There is plenty an individual must still do to turn a genetic inheritance into worldly triumph. **"It is the temperament of a revolutionary that is genetic,"** he wrote. **"What an individual does with his biology is up to him."**

John F. Kennedy had several hypomanic traits. One of his biographers, William Manchester, wrote that he would "vibrate with energy. He would pace corridors, read on his feet, dictate rapidly, dart out for brisk constitutionals around the monument, and return in a sprint, snapping his restless fingers." Kennedy's restless physical movement occasionally resulted in farce. "Two White House chairs have collapsed under the stress. Once . . . in the middle of a conference with congressional leaders . . . he was fidgeting away, and the next moment there was an explosion, a hail of ancient splinters, and a loud thump as the Chief Executive sprawled at the feet of his astonished Vice-President." A contemporary profile of Kennedy in *The New Republic* titled "The Mind of JFK" reported that "There is nothing he dislikes more, it is testified, than a nice, orderly day with five appointments neatly spaced. . . . [H]e keeps filling in the gaps in the appointment list until he has guaranteed himself a twelve-appointment day of continuous action . . .[s]harp, drift-free tuning which permits movement from one problem to another without overlap or confusion . . . [a]n unflagging intent of action. A zest which confers absurdity upon all the melodramatic and maudlin folklore about the loneliness, anguish, and burdens of the presidency."

Even as a young senator, those around him complained of his speed and recklessness. His secretary, Evelyn Lincoln, said he only left for airplane flights at the last possible minute. And then Kennedy liked to "take the wheel and race through the streets, barely missing red lights. Cops would whistle, cars would honk, but he ignored everything. . . . Muggsie [his driver] . . . would invariably report that they pulled away the steps to the plane as soon as the Senator climbed on. . . I fully expected to get a call someday with the news that they had failed to make one of those curves on their way to National Airport."

Kennedy's hyperactivity revealed his sheer enthusiasm for life, a trait we see in many successful people. Sir Richard Branson, the founder of the Virgin group, once explained his own taste for physical danger and business adventures: "I live life to the full in a lot of different areas so I'm learning all the time. I've seen life as one long learning experience . . . I have an absolute fascination for every aspect of life. I'm open to ideas." When he was in high school, his headmaster told him he was either going to be a millionaire or end up in jail. He achieved the former many times over and flirted with the latter during the many lawsuits that he fought and won early in his career.

Branson, like Kennedy, was never constrained by conformity or rules, which he felt got in the way of great ideas. As his longtime lieutenant Will Whitehorn told *The New Yorker*: "Richard is highly intelligent but educationally dyslexic. It has forced him to live by his gut reaction to things, and that has served him well. I was brought up in a more academic environment—to find there was always a reason why something can't happen. Richard hates it when people tell him that. He isn't hamstrung by academic disputes. He finds them tedious."

A story from the founding of Virgin Atlantic Airways illustrates Branson's determination to buck convention in pursuit of good business. He was a record executive who found himself stuck in the British Virgin Islands after his flight to Puerto Rico was canceled. Rather than stewing in the departure lounge, he called around and found a company that would charter him a jet for $2,000. He then divided the price by the number of seats, borrowed a blackboard, and wrote "Virgin Airways, $39 single flight to Puerto Rico." As he later recalled, "I walked around the terminal and soon filled every seat on the plane."

When former U.S. military analyst, David Ellsberg, released the Pentagon Papers in 1961, he provided strong evidence that **decision makers dislike ambiguity, but entrepreneurs usually thrive in**

ambiguous situations. Some individuals abhor ambiguity/risks and attempt to minimize them; entrepreneurs are attracted to risky situations and thrive when confronted with uncertainty.

College students, I believe, require two kinds of education: one that serves them well in the marketplace and one that helps them consider the meaning of life. Often, they receive too much of the former and not enough of the latter. Without understanding the meaning of life, comparative values alter over time. Time, says Sophocles, takes many things which once were pleasures and brings them nearer to pain. "In the day when the strong men shall bow themselves, and desire shall fail, it will be a matter of yet more concern than now, whether one can say, 'My mind to me a kingdom is'; and whether the windows of the soul look out upon a broad and delightful landscape, or face nothing but a brick wall."

This is different from faith, which is also crucial. The meaning of life is not faith. It's understanding and integrating loyalty, patience, respect and help for others, honesty, duty, integrity, humility, gratitude, fairness, generosity, caring, kindness, truthfulness, and growth.

People said of me as a college president, "You're running the institution like a business."

I'd respond, "No, the output of a business is money and the output of an education is the acquisition of skills and an understanding of the meaning of life." A college is not a business, because the output is not quantifiable.

My own life has been one of constant balancing and rebalancing, of trying to marry my professional and personal goals. It has been a life typical for an entrepreneur and one, I hope, worthy of sharing.

ALWAYS REMEMBER:

- Master your own destiny and solve problems for others.

- The status quo is never satisfactory, it must be changed.

- You and your organization must dance to forms of music now unheard.

- All progress depends on the unreasonable man.

- Ambiguity is your friend for it provides options and opportunities.

ONE

LAYING A FOUNDATION

"If wishes were horses, the beggars would ride."
—Kathleen Cosgrove Douglas, my mother

"I've lived through dreaming and not having, and I've lived through having. The basic substance, to me, is still getting up in the morning and feeling good about yourself—I don't care how rich you are."
—Ralph Lauren

I was born on Friday, January 13, in the depths of the Great Depression. My father, Benjamin Douglas, said it was the 13th day of the 13th month—the day the banks closed. It was not a propitious start.

Pop was born to the purple. His father had owned a successful construction company that had built the first train tunnel under the Detroit River to Windsor, and married Margaretta Biddle, from a wealthy Philadelphia family. He had grown up on an estate on Grosse Ile, on the Detroit River, playing tennis, sailing, and enjoying all that money could buy. But when he was 13, his life took a sudden and tragic turn: His father fell off a railroad bridge he had built in Brazil.

For a while, Pop's life carried on as usual. He trained as a chemical engineer, took the European Grand Tour after college, and married my mother, Kathleen Cosgrove, in 1927. But when the Depression came and wiped out most of their assets, Pop was not prepared. He had always disdained hard work and money, an unfortunate trait often found in those born rich.

For Pop, accumulating assets had no redeeming social value whatsoever. So when his legacy was wiped out in the Depression, rather than seeking to rebuild it, he closed his eyes to reality. His childhood had not prepared him to be resilient. He felt aggrieved that he was no longer wealthy and resented the petty indignities of having to scrape by. He would try to console himself and us by saying, "We're not poor, just broke," as if, despite everything, we were still somehow special. But even at an early age, I knew there was no hiding it: We had no money.

For a while my father sought an intellectual hiding place in socialism and the Technocracy Movement, which argued that engineers should rule the world. But technocracy fell victim to critics like Winston Churchill, who eviscerated the movement's central belief in one sentence: "We want a lot of engineers in the world, but we do not want a world of engineers."

Pop eventually went back to college and retrained as a junior high school English teacher. His wages were paid in script during the Depression, redeemable for food at the local grocery store. As a family, we knew we weren't going to starve, but there was not much left over. Had I known anything different, I might have felt oppressed, but it was just our way of life.

At this point my father embraced socialism, as did we. We were sent to the camps and taught "give each according to his need, take from each according to his ability to pay." We sang the songs and heard the doctrine. However, socialism takes away your willingness and interest in excelling, competing, and leading to a better life.

My mother was quite different. She never took adversity lying down. As the daughter of a Presbyterian minister, she had grown up in the genteel poverty that clerics typically endured. She was a teacher and librarian, a smart woman and a businessperson. Although it was painful for her, given my father's attitude toward money, she kept the family's books. It was left to her to keep body and soul together and to see that the family remained afloat. Luckily for my father, despite everything, she really loved him.

In 1941, when I was eight years old, we moved within Michigan from a house in Pleasant Ridge to an old rundown farmhouse on ten acres near Birmingham. In financial terms, it wasn't a smart move. My father had to drive 60 miles a day to school and back at a time when gas was rationed. And our house needed a lot of work and money. Although there was a furnace, it only forced heat through a register in the center of the dining room at the middle of the house, leaving the rest of the house to freeze. My parents installed a steam heating system, but it didn't provide hot water in the summertime. The sanitary disposal system turned out to be a line run across adjacent property with open joints—there was no city sanitary sewer, septic tank, or treatment facility. We weren't poor, just broke; we had vision and opportunities but no money.

Fortunately, my mother's genius for survival shone through all our difficulties. We grew a lot of vegetables on the farm. We had lima beans, and we shelled them and put them in jars for later. While they weren't very good when we stored them, my mother always said, "They'll taste better than snowballs next winter." We would pick wild blackberries and strawberries, and she would put them in boxes and sell them.

We were always trying to find a way to make ends meet, and my mother encouraged all of us children to work from a young age. She motivated us to strive and, unlike my father, was never "broke" in a spiritual or emotional sense. Quite the opposite. Life was rarely easy for her, but she never lost her self-respect, or failed to impress the importance of hard work and self-confidence on her children. She also stressed our heritage, the Biddles, the Douglas who was head of the Michigan Supreme Court, the construction people who had accomplished outstanding feats, and the like.

I remember once driving with her at high speed in her car. A policeman stopped us. He put his foot on the running board and said, "You exceeded the speed limit. You shouldn't drive like that with a young boy in your car. It's not safe."

She replied that he could write her a ticket but not speak to her disrespectfully as though she were a slow child.

The officer kept on talking until my mother put her car in gear and took off. He overhauled her, cut her off, and silently wrote her a ticket. As we drove away, she said to me, "That's a life lesson. They can write you a ticket, but they can't lecture you."

IGNORE THE NAYSAYERS

The world is full of people who tell you what not to do: governmental authorities, engineers who haven't learned the latest design skills, and others. You must look them in the eye and say they can't lecture to you; you see the future and it is bright and clear.

Ours was an environment in which we were called to learn, grow, and excel, regardless of financial resources.

From as young as I can remember, I was expected to have a job and earn money. My parents wanted me not only to work but to save. They stressed the importance of going to college, but they also told me if I didn't work and have the money, I would never go. Before and during my high school years, I worked so many different jobs I've since lost count of them all.

One hot summer, when I was ten, I worked on a hay baler, tying the wires. It was difficult, especially when I was ill with hay fever and had to work with runny eyes and an itchy nose. At the end of the season, my employer gave me a pig as payment. My mother took it to be processed and packaged and put it in the freezer for us to eat. When I was 12, I worked for a guy who raised gladiolas. The work involved planting, weeding, and cultivating, and then selling the flowers on the street corner. I also worked for a man who grew tarragon; I weeded, cultivated, and picked the plants.

I had a newspaper route and would deliver papers on the one-mile stretch from school to home. This job taught me how to deal with customers and collect payments. I found there were three kinds of people who bought the papers. One person would meet me at the door and willingly give me the money. One person would meet me at the door and tell me why he or she couldn't give me the money but promised to pay me later. The third person just hid out in the back and wouldn't answer the door. I have since had clients in all those categories.

I also mowed lawns. My father and I bought a tractor when I was in high school, and in addition to mowing, I used the tractor to plow the snow on the city sidewalks. I plowed gardens—almost everyone had a garden—and maintained the baseball field. My father and I were in business together, although we had very different approaches to the work. Pop didn't like to think about money and would spend all of his time talking to people. I focused on the work that had to be done and the money I needed to collect.

I learned the most basic elements of business during that time: show up on time; keep working whatever the weather or the status of your health; and be part of what is going on, whether you are directly involved or not.

One day, when I was 16, my father came to me and said, "I have a scholarship for you to act in the plays at Cranbrook Academy this summer." Cranbrook was one of Michigan's top private schools, three or four miles away from home but a world away from the education I had known.

"How can I do that? I'm working at Pontiac Motor," I said to my father.

"Which shift do you work?"

"I can pick any shift."

"Okay. Just work from midnight until seven thirty in the morning and then come home, shower, and go to Cranbrook."

And that is what I did for a couple of summers. It was a farrago. All night long, I was on the assembly line, doing mindless work alongside blue-collar types with no aspirations or future. In the morning, I was on stage with the cutest, richest girls around. I met some nice women, so it wasn't all bad. But neither the factory life nor the pampered life was right for me, and I wasn't much good as an actor. What I knew by my late teens was that I liked making money and saving money and having enough to know I could go to college. Everything else, I figured, would work itself out.

MASTER OF MY OWN FATE

Growing up in the Depression, I formed certain habits that have stayed with me throughout my life. I became self-sufficient, both financially and emotionally. Watching the differing responses of my father and mother to our difficulties, I realized my fate lay entirely in my own hands. I learned how hard it is to earn a dollar and have never lost my respect for those who do. I became resourceful and creative about making money. And I learned the importance of the simple things, doing what you say you will do, and ensuring you get paid for it.

I scarcely knew it at the time, but I was developing the basic traits of an entrepreneur. But was it nature or nurture pushing me in this direction? My mother certainly had a strong sense that we were genetically blessed. She taught us about our family history on both sides and instilled in us the belief that we were born to succeed. She was the one who told us about my father's father, who had made his fortune in construction, and relative Samuel Douglas, the Chief Justice of the Michigan Supreme Court. Justice Douglas was famous for saying there were three cases presented by a lawyer in every trial in court: the one you prepared, the one you actually gave, and the one you thought of on the way home. My paternal grandmother also had a remarkable family, the Biddles of Philadelphia, whom mother researched assiduously. I remember her telling me: "You have the genealogy and heritage to do whatever you want, and you have some great people in this family at various points along the way."

This affected me so profoundly that, decades later, when I had to choose a subject for my doctoral dissertation, I wrote about an uncle six generations back, Nicholas Biddle, who was head of the Second Bank of the United States. I believed he had been mistreated by history, portrayed as a man who had a dangerous effect on inflation, money supply, and the price of gold. I felt I could fix his reputation, and I did. Call it an entrepreneurial approach to historiography.

It was apparent that long before psychologists began studying the brain patterns of entrepreneurs, my mother was convinced the achievements and behaviors of our ancestors predicted our own. But she was also a stern believer in self-improvement. **There was no use inheriting great genes if you did nothing with them.** She pushed me to overcome the limitations of my school, where most students were only interested in athletics, and to devote my energy to studying hard. I was a state spelling bee champion in grade school. It wasn't hard to be good at school because the teachers were poorly educated and easily satisfied. But I did the best I could and did especially well in math and science. Looking back, I wish my parents had tried to find a way to send me to Cranbrook to better prepare me for college. I wasn't well schooled. It was ironic that my two educated parents left me to languish in a substandard school. Perhaps it wasn't financially feasible for me to go to a private school, but as a parent I would have found a way.

My experience at school left me with a permanent desire to learn more, to close the gap I felt opened up during those early years. It made me a lifelong student, which has served me well, but I would rather have chosen the path instead of being forced onto it. A poor secondary education can create a hunger for knowledge.

My father fueled my ambition in a very different way. He was aloof, acerbic, and difficult. When I tried to speak to him about any matter he talked over me to blank out what I wanted to say. He did that with almost everyone. He would say to others he was proud of something I had done, and they would pass it on, but that was the only way I ever received praise. And he wasn't admirable in a physical sense—he was fat, he smoked, and he was disorderly. His dirty automobile was not a place you wanted to be.

One time, when I was a young person, I asked him for money to go out to a party. He reluctantly reached in his pocket and gave me a few dollars, then growled about it until I left. I never asked again.

It was clear to me I was going to be on my own at an early age; in my case, at about 16. That was made easier by my father's distance from the family. Though school ended at 3:00 p.m., Pop never came home until 6:00 p.m. He spent the afternoons in a friend's drugstore, spending money my mother gave him out of our meager family funds.

Yet there are influences that need to be explained. I've always been interested in education, leading me to two postgraduate degrees later in life. I would eventually volunteer to be responsible for a class of inner-city children whom we put through high school and college. I became a university trustee for two institutions for a total of 20 years and served as a college president.

What does all that mean? Can you posit that my father directed me in that fashion, gave me a vector for education? Perhaps. Or was it pure accident? Unlikely.

Every son's father has a notable effect on him. Mine certainly did—in a positive and a negative way. There were the daily arguments when we were running the tractor business. I wanted to do the work and perform better than anyone else, while he wanted to talk with

41

the people we were serving. I can't tell you the number of times that the whole family was waiting in the automobile to return home while my father was out talking to someone else for an extended period of time. We'd almost have to grab him and pull him into the car so we could leave.

He was prone to making unnecessary cutting remarks. When I was in high school, I remember him telling me he was denied a number of things in his life but that some of them he would have "after the kids get through college." Since he was not planning to financially support me through college, that seemed a little mean-spirited to me.

As free as he was with criticism, the opposite was true of compliments. Early in high school when I was a 120-pound football player, he spoke with the coach and was told there was concern I might break some of my bones if I played in a football game. I played pretty well: I earned a letter and didn't break anything. But still, Pop never complimented me on my ability.

Successful entrepreneurs are often said to have shown great tenacity and skill on the sports field. I was not one of them. I was mediocre in basketball, baseball, and football, though I earned letters in sports. But I did learn a few things that have stuck with me. I recall playing second base in high school when the guy at first tried to steal second. When the catcher threw the ball to me, I caught it but missed the tag on the runner. When he slid past second, I jumped on him, but still missed him coming back. After the inning, as we came off the field, my coach said to me, **"Let me tell you something that you'll remember all your life: Never make a second stab. Don't expend extra effort in a futile cause after you've lost. Most often, when you try to do something again after you've done it wrong, you'll just make it worse."**

It's not the sort of "leave it all on the field" lesson most people get from sports, but it made sense to me then and has ever since. This piece of advice is particularly applicable to real estate development. In that endeavor you can't make a good deal with a bad person, and expending extraordinary effort to get the four pieces in line—site selection, financing, leasing, and management—can be futile if your partner is not worthy.

All those years working and saving allowed me to attend Kalamazoo College to earn a BA in physics and move on to the University of Michigan to earn a BS in civil engineering. But I never stopped making my own money throughout college. I shoveled coal in the school boiler room and represented a laundry and dry cleaner, going around campus picking up and delivering clothes. Working your way through college may be virtuous, but you miss a lot of opportunities for education and emotional growth in the process.

I just held a reunion for Kalamazoo College graduates at our home in Florida. When the president asked me to relate my experiences at Kalamazoo, I said those three years from 1950 to 1953 weren't easy, since I struggled academically, worked all the time, and got dumped by my girlfriend in my junior year. Also, the physics professor I came to study under died in my freshman year. Still, hard as it was, it was the right choice. My father had suggested I could learn engineering quickly but that what I needed was a liberal arts education—philosophy, religion, languages, literature, and the like—before more technical studies.

At the University of Michigan, in engineering school, I worked for a professor setting up laboratories and grading papers. At a sorority house, I waited tables in exchange for a meal. It was a poor deal. The women took an hour and a half to eat and then the least attractive girl in the house asked me to the pledge formals. At a fraternity, I was the assistant cook. That was barter too, but the young men only spent 20 minutes eating and then were gone.

Two great things happened for me at college. First, I graduated top of my class at Michigan.

Second, and much more significantly, I met Dolores, or Dee, who would become my wife.

We met on a blind date. A buddy of mine was dating a nurse, and he arranged for me to meet her friend, who was studying nursing at Nazareth College. My buddy was a nerd, so even as I went along with his plan, my hopes weren't high. I thought the date wouldn't amount to much. Happily, I was wrong.

Thinking back to my life leading up to graduation, it was scarcely one of boundless opportunity and luxury. It was filled with hard work, with no room for idling. My dreams were still unformed, and I knew little of the world beyond what I had grown up with in Michigan.

But my habits, both professional and personal, had taken shape: I knew I could apply the effort both mentally and physically to overcome challenges. I had been around a lot of people from different backgrounds and had become a good judge of character. I had pressed my nose up against the windows into privileged worlds, without being let in. I had met a woman as sensible as I could ever hope to marry.

I didn't realize it at the time, but all of my actions and experiences were laying the foundation for my subsequent career as an entrepreneur. Once I found what I wanted to do with my life, I was confident I could achieve any goals.

TRAITS OF AN ENTREPRENEUR

I clearly had the traits of an entrepreneur, courtesy of my genes and my experiences as a boy. Not every boy growing up as I did might have been so determined to change his circumstances. The men I knew on the assembly line had resigned themselves to theirs. But as I examine my life, I can see my response to every kind of adversity was what we might call, for want of a better word, entrepreneurial. I responded to my dissatisfaction with a determination to make things better. I developed those habits I believed I needed to succeed. I imagined a life and experiences far beyond my present condition.

Therein, I believe, lies the balance between nature and nurture. Nature is a gift that can set you up well—or not. It is a stone to be polished through nurture, and the harder you polish, the more brightly that gift will shine.

Taking a close look at yourself and being honest about your desires and your will to achieve them is the first step to becoming a successful entrepreneur. The next step is the hard work of bringing them into reality.

ALWAYS REMEMBER:

- You may be broke but you're not poor, vision and opportunities are more important than money.

- When faced with naysayers or disciplinarians, they can write you a ticket but they can't lecture to you.

- Both nature and nurture are important for your progress as an entrepreneur.

- Never make a second stab, don't spend extra effort in a futile cause after you've lost.

TWO

GETTING GOING

"The great pleasure in life is doing what
people say you cannot do."
—Walter Bagehot

One of the greatest mysteries of entrepreneurship is how careers get started in the first place. Anyone who wants to start their own business is faced with dozens of choices. What industry to go into? Where to secure financing? Whom to hire? How to get that first customer? How to build trust and a reputation?

By the time I left college, I knew I wanted to work in the construction business. I liked all the pieces and parts of it, the mathematical challenge, and the engineering. I always cared about how things went together and worked. It still fascinates me.

But being interested is only a start.

Back in the 1950s, there wasn't much demand for engineers. People would tell me, "You don't want to be an engineer. There's not a market for engineers." But I believed that if I could become a good engineer, I'd be successful. There were opportunities, and I began seeking them out.

I told my father I wanted to speak with the heads of the main construction companies in Detroit and asked him, "Will I have trouble getting in to talk to the presidents of those companies?"

He said, "Your problem won't be getting in. Your problem will be getting out."

He was right; they were happy I was interested in their business. Not many students were. And I listened carefully to what they had to say. They offered all sorts of advice, ranging from the kind of personality I would need to succeed to what I needed to complete my formal education.

I had an uncle, Gilbert Douglas, who owned a company working mainly in commercial construction, and while I wasn't exceptionally close to him, I went to see him, and he influenced me greatly. He became one of my earliest mentors in the business. Of course, not everything he told me sank in. **He warned me I should never put money into a company I didn't control, and it was a lesson I had to learn later through a mistake**. It provided a bitter experience.

Through those conversations, I came to understand what I would and would not enjoy about construction. What engaged me most were the ideas and the designs, the crafting of deals and seeing difficult projects through to their completion. Standing on a building site and pounding my chest importantly as the jackhammers and drills thundered was not going to be for me.

When I graduated from Michigan, the Pennsylvania Railroad people invited the top two civil engineers to Philadelphia, of which I was one. When we arrived they said to my friend and me, "Go down the hall and take a physical." Unlike our interviews at other companies, we never met with a key executive of the railroad. When I got back to Ann Arbor there was a letter telling me where to report to work and what my salary would be.

That's no way to treat an entrepreneur. Working in that environment was a bad idea, and I rejected the job.

After the University of Michigan, I spent time on the Indiana Turnpike. In the mornings I ran a survey party for the design company, in the afternoons a concrete crew. One day the boss of Western Construction came in to my little hut as I was completing my concrete records for the day.

He said, "Come with me."

We took off in his car down the right of way through the dust and mud. The person who had my job in the next segment of the road had failed to adjust the device that formed the pavement surface, called a screed, to reinstitute the crown when he came out of a super-elevated curve. They had paved a mile of the highway flat and now had to tear it out and replace it.

We walked into the hut where my opposite number was doing his work, and the boss said, "Do you have a box? Get all of your stuff in it and be out of here in 10 minutes."

We got back in the car and were heading east along the roadway when the man said, "There's a lesson for you."

It certainly was.

Before I could truly embark on my chosen career, I did what most men of my generation did and joined the armed forces. Dee and I were married in October 1955. By Thanksgiving, I was attending the Navy Officer's Candidate School in Rhode Island, and Dee was one month pregnant, working the night shift in a Boston hospital and living in her brother's unheated attic. It was a tough start to married life.

If you ask Dee about her military career, you get a grim story: a pregnancy in Boston; the birth of a child in the military hospital in Port Hueneme, California; arriving in Japan with a month-old baby to be greeted by an earthquake; life in isolation on the Japanese countryside; the loss of a child at the same military hospital two years later; and the difficulty of being a shy girl in a naval officer's world. I thought I was taking a girl from a potato and onion farm to see the world, but she saw it differently.

On the way to the gym a few days ago Dee said to me, "You're a very intelligent person. Why did you marry me?"

I've always told her it was because she had great legs and curly hair, and I repeated that. She said there had to be more to it than that—and there was, much more.

When I asked my father about marriage he gave no advice, just as he had when I was selecting a college, and said I was basically on my own. He was proud of me as a naval officer, though, and visited the base in California where I was stationed.

My first job in the Navy after Officer's Candidate School was to troll through universities in Michigan and Ohio to find recruits for the school. Even though the Korean War had ended, military service was not a popular choice for college kids. I remember driving in a parade at the University of Michigan in a convertible painted with the Naval insignia and later hearing the laughs and heckles from students at the Pretzel Bell, a popular college drinking hole. I cared enough about what I was doing to press on, **but the experience taught me the importance of not putting yourself in a position of easy ridicule if you want to get things done.**

Next, I was sent on an eight-week program in civil engineering to prepare me to lead engineering projects in and around two major Navy bases in Japan, at Yokosuka, in Tokyo Bay. Up to this point in my life, I hadn't given much thought to the mechanics of leadership and management. I knew I wanted to go into construction, but what interested me most was the engineering and problem solving. It was the Navy that forced me to learn that leading people is just as much of a challenge.

You manage things and you lead people,
not the reverse.

My work involved building everything from housing to piers to sea walls and the docks used by submarines. I had a boat for the submarine base we remodeled, an airplane for housing projects inland, and a diving suit to check the progress of seawall construction and other underwater projects. It would have taken me years to acquire similar responsibilities and experiences in the private sector. It turned out to be ideal training for an entrepreneur.

There's a lot to learn if you're a naval officer. My neighbor on the base ran the ship store. He told me a story of a Turkish sailor who bought a camera, took it outside the gate, and sold it on the black market. When the Turks were called in to see the apprehended sailor the officer asked, "Did he confess?"

When told he had not, he put his gun on the table and asked to be left alone with the man. The officer told him he wouldn't shoot him there because it would be embarrassing to the US Navy but would take him back to the ship to shoot him. The Turkish sailor confessed in 10 minutes.

That's discipline.

I was lucky to be given a lot of control over my projects by the Navy. More, perhaps, than a man my age should have had. I started as a resident officer in charge of construction in Yokosuka, Japan, at the Navy base, a position that allowed me to challenge the traditional chain of command.

My staff was 15 Japanese engineers with military background (the chief had been an admiral in the Japanese navy). Leading this crew took technical skill and a sense of humor. A decade on from the Second World War, the US Navy was still suspicious of the Japanese, and any Japanese who came to work on the bases was subjected to a complicated pass procedure. This made my job difficult. If projects were going slowly, it was hard to hire new workers because of all the extra paperwork involved in getting them on and off the base. Equally, I was under great pressure to get these projects finished. Failure was not an option.

Eventually, I had enough of it and told my Japanese contractors: "Bring a boat in here at midnight with a bunch of people and to hell with the pass procedure."

The next morning, another twenty men showed up, and while we never got the pass part of it straightened out, I did get my additional workers, who moved into temporary barracks on the base. An entrepreneur's mindset must be "land your boats on the enemy's beach and burn them, go forward to your objective." You can't turn back.

Not being allowed to fail can be a great spur to creativity and action.

I was once overseeing a project on the submarine base when my commander decided to make changes by speaking directly to the Japanese contractor. I was furious.

"Stay off my job," I told him. "You don't get to make these decisions on this work. I'm in charge and you're just not supposed to do things like that."

At the end of the call, he was quiet. That night, I went out drinking with a friend and told him what I had done. We agreed that I was in deep trouble.

But the next morning as I was shaving, the commander called me. "You know, I'm headed for Pearl Harbor and I just wanted to tell you, you were right. I shouldn't have come on your job site and made changes."

Despite his apology, I realized I had been disrespectful and said, "I think I made a damn fool of myself. There are other ways to express concern. I didn't do it properly."

"Just keep up the work," he told me. "I know you feel strongly about these sorts of things."

That is leadership. You'd take bullets for a guy like that, who
supports your efforts and is humble enough to listen and realize
when he's wrong.

LEARN TO LISTEN

Just as my commander listened to me, I learned to listen to
others. My captain in Japan, who ran construction all across the
Far East, gave me a great piece of advice early in my tour: "You
have two chief petty officers who report to you, and if you go to
those two guys and tell them you don't know how to do your job,
they'll look after you, take care of you, and you'll have a good
tour of duty."

So, I took those two guys to a bar and said, "I really don't know
how to do this job, and I need your help."

They'd already figured that out.

I told them: "I want to be successful here. I want to learn. I
want everything to go well, and I'd appreciate your help."

Sure enough, they looked after me and helped me. I've continued doing that all my life.

Also on my staff was a Japanese engineer who had been a subma-
riner in the Japanese submarine navy. He was knowledgeable and had
a great sense of humor. I'd go to him and say, "What do you think,
Itoh-san? How should we solve this problem? What should we do?"

He was able to tell me what he thought, and I was able to learn
and grow as a result.

Entrepreneurs excel in cross-linking and rearranging information
in ways that lead them to new projects. Don Y. Lee and Eric W.

K. Tsang investigated the effects of different entrepreneurial personalities upon success among 168 Chinese entrepreneurs in Singapore and found that those who had strong leads for specific achievable goals were most successful. Those who were strongly self-reliant or extroverted were less successful. Their findings suggest successful entrepreneurs must believe they control their own destinies and, at the same time, not become too self-reliant.

The ability to seek out and accept assistance from others at appropriate times is a key to success.

As I responded to that small young man at the engineering leadership lecture, who asked for the key to making lots of money, it was the mentors I had that were the key to my successes. That will always be true in any number of endeavors; for instance, without Dr. James Fisher or Dr. John Silber, my academic career would not have been possible.

STUDY THE PERSON

Wayne Huizenga took three humble business ideas and created Fortune 500 companies: Waste Management, Blockbuster Entertainment, and AutoNation. He's not an inventor but an entrepreneur. If you took away everything he has—financial resources, management team, money, the keys to his car—and put him in a one-bedroom apartment in downtown Miami, a multibillion dollar Fortune 500 company would likely burst out of that room. Wayne had that genetic orientation and a great desire. It's better to study the person than the idea, because the individual can make a business model work.

The reason most entrepreneurs founded their own
firms is that they wanted to change something–perhaps how
products are made, how they are marketed and sold,
or how and where they are used.

Psychologist Edwin Locke said that the entrepreneurs he calls prime movers are enormously ambitious. They differ from other people in the scope and intensity of their ambitions. Entrepreneurs are likely to stir things up in their organizations; they are much more change oriented than other CEOs. Richard Kovocevich, CEO of Wells Fargo Bank, perceived the difference between managers and leaders: Managers rely on systems; leaders rely on people. Managers work on getting things right; leaders work on the right things. Peter Drucker agreed that effectiveness is more important than efficiency.

Transformational CEOs tend to be leaders who have a propensity to
divert or go around organizational structures and deal directly with
key people in order to accomplish change.

Remember, if you enjoy stirring things up, frequently think outside the box, generate lots of innovative ideas, frequently violate the status quo, often obviate the chain of command, and do not strongly believe in organizational structures, then you are much more likely to become an entrepreneur. Behavioral genetics evidence indicates these characteristics appear to be heritable. Everyday life tends to sort out entrepreneurial individuals, who self-select roles and occupations where they can exercise their entrepreneurial inclinations.

Entrepreneurs bring something new to the game based on genealogy, enthusiasm, and intense desire. With that heredity, an engineer can find himself in a position where he sees what can be done with the resources at hand and says, "I can change that for the better." Henry Ford didn't invent the automobile. He invented a way to manufacture and sell cars to middle-class people.

So much of business is about finding the best way to a solution.

Sometimes that will involve going around the normal procedures to find the right person. I remember working on sea walls at the Yokosuka base in Japan and having to make a lot of changes. The normal procedure for making these changes would have been to slog through the chain of command for approval. But on this occasion I learned there was a guy in the public works department named Roy Guilland who could issue authorizations much more quickly. Understanding these hidden organizational maps, and building relationships so that you can navigate them, is vital to success. Some might call this breaking the chain of command. I would call it making things happen, and I've been doing it all my life.

But on other occasions I understood that the formal procedures existed for a reason. It was a custom in the Navy to pay social calls on superior officers at home. You stopped by with your wife, dropped your card in a silver tray at the door, spent 20 minutes paying your respects, and left. By doing this, I got to know the admiral for whom I was building a tennis facility in Yokosuka. We would play tennis together, and he would then come to our house in the country to reciprocate, drink all my Scotch and stay until two in the morning. It turned out to be a valuable relationship—for all kinds of reasons.

One day Dee asked me to drive her brother to the airport in Los Angeles from Port Hueneme. My vehicle was an old MG with poor brakes, which broke down on the way home. I was the officer of the day, as well, and not supposed to leave the base. When I returned after driving with the emergency brake and downshifting, we were scheduled for a party at the admiral's home.

When I walked in, he said, "Young man, you look like you could use a drink."

I said, "I'm not allowed to drink since I am the OOD." I didn't tell him I'd already been off the base, inappropriately, for the bulk of the day.

He handed me a glass. "Here. You can drink."

It was a relief.

The Navy believed they could make anybody into an effective leader—and a naval officer. I was very lucky the Navy gave me the experiences and responsibilities it did. Among the vital lessons I learned there was the importance of expertise. It was hard work staying in Officer Candidate School. Around half of my section of 35 were dismissed, many because they couldn't master navigation. But my interest in mathematics carried me through. I enjoyed the engineering aspects of the Navy, and this gave me confidence in other areas.

> People will only trust you if they believe you
> know what you're doing.

The Navy also forced me to take command and complete projects without all the information or expertise I might have wanted. This was vital in developing my self-confidence. I learned the importance of working scared, standing up for myself, but also of listening to my peers and subordinates and caring for them as people. I learned to communicate with people at every level.

If I had been egocentric and arrogant, this wouldn't have worked. It was hard for a young guy to go to people who worked for him and say, "I'm trying to figure this out, help me." But now I've been doing that all my life. When I became president of a college in my 70s, I would go to faculty and vice presidents and say, "I don't fully understand. I really want to listen. I want you to tell me what you think is right for students. I'll learn and we'll do this together."

My habit was to walk around the campus and drop in on professors in their offices. I'd learn about their discipline, ask for the loan of a book, and talk about college affairs. The respect generated by this process provided cohesion within the college and obviated faculty unrest. Many college presidents suffer votes of "no confidence" from their faculty because they're autocratic and aloof. Though I changed a lot at the school, including the faculty governance system, that possibility never was a threat. The Navy taught me that skill and taught me to understand that "command and control," issuing orders without feedback, doesn't always work.

But the Navy also reinforced my desire to go it alone. I realized that if I stayed in the Navy, I'd always be in conflict with others about what we did and the scope of my authority. It would have taken me years to rise through the ranks, especially since I hadn't attended the Naval Academy. Also, I wanted to make some money. I wanted to support my family and not need for my wife to work. Ultimately, I was more interested in the technical aspects of design and construction, and creating my own business, than fighting my way through the Navy's politics and bureaucracy. Like many entrepreneurs, I was never going to be happy working for others.

It was time to put all this learning to work for myself.

Machiavelli said that people would judge you on what you appear to be, rather than who you are. Yet it's who you are that matters.

ALWAYS REMEMBER:

- Assume the attitude that if you don't reach your goals through intense focus, you will literally die.

- Plan and manage your business and your life with passion and precision.

- Look to others for assistance and guidance, including people who work for you that care about your business and your future.

THREE

LURCHING ALONG

"An organization is just the lengthened
shadow of a single man."
—Ralph Waldo Emerson

Experience and capital are the two building blocks of a start-up. When I left the Navy, I had experience but no capital. Our savings were meager, and I now had a young family to support. Dee, fortunately, has always been even thriftier than I. We've never spent more than we've earned, and this has allowed me to take risks which might have been beyond anyone saddled with expenses.

After the Navy, I returned to Ohio to work for F. W. Entenman, a construction company in Toledo, as a project manager and estimator. I still had much to learn and many gaps in my knowledge to fill. By working hard and developing mentors, I acquired what I needed: knowledge of the business side of construction.

I learned as much about how to manage as how not to.

One of my bosses was a man named Hector MacKinnon. I remember once building a warehouse for Johns Manville in Defiance, Ohio. This was a project won because we implemented new structural design techniques and others didn't. One day, the company's managers came and asked me to give them a price for adding 40,000 square feet to another of their buildings. I worked on the proposal all night and gave it to them the next morning. They sent me a purchase order. But as we started the work I realized I had overestimated the cost and that our profit would be substantially more than we expected.

I went to MacKinnon and suggested we give them back $20,000.

He refused.

I told him, "If we don't, I quit."

I was in no position to look for another job, since Dee was pregnant again, we were living in an apartment, driving an old car, and had little money in the bank. MacKinnon, to his credit, told me that if I believed that strongly about it I could give the money back, though I was not obliged to do so. I returned the money.

After that, we built for Johns Manville in various parts of the country, and I was always introduced as the man who returned money when it wasn't required. That had been the right thing to do, and it fostered a relationship that led to additional projects.

My success at Entenman led to an offer from a rival company, Lathrop, which promised more money and larger opportunities. And not least, I could work as a superintendent, the on-site manager directing the work. It was experience I lacked and badly wanted.

As a construction superintendent, you show up early in the morning, clean, ready to work and with a list of things you want to get done that day. By 10 or 11 in the morning, all kinds of problems have developed, and the work on your list gets displaced by the crisis of the moment. It didn't take me long to learn to function on a moment-by-moment basis.

My first project as a superintendent was a warehouse that I had bid for Owens-Illinois, a glassmaker headquartered in Toledo, at a new plant in Charlotte, Michigan. I was given a pickup truck, equipment, and supplies, and I found a local secretary to handle the paperwork. The work was challenging, and I constantly pushed myself. There was so much I wanted to learn—particularly about tools, processes, quality control, and problem solving. **Having a list of what you want to learn is important.** It was a great experience, and the project came out well.

At the start of the project, Dee came with me and lived in a rented cottage on Duck Lake. She scarcely saw me. I left at six in the morning and returned at nine in the evening. Partway through the summer Dee had had enough, and she took the children and went back to Toledo. By that time she was pregnant with our third child. Ever since, we've stayed together in the same place during all my projects, but **finding the right balance between work and family— especially early in my career—was always a challenge.**

Selling and sales relationships were still new to me. The president of Lathrop was an excellent salesman, and whenever I asked clients why they kept coming back to Lathrop, even when its costs were higher than its rivals, they said it was the relationship. Everyone at Lathrop knew this and worked diligently to nurture their relationships with customers and suppliers.

Eventually, the moment came for me to leave. I'd saved enough money and felt confident I was ready to start up on my own. I went to my boss and handed in my notice.

He said, "Okay. You can be out of here this afternoon."

The only problem was I was in the middle of a project for a local manufacturing company. I told my boss I'd be happy to spend at least a couple of weeks ensuring the plans were laid out clearly and helping my successor. He said it wasn't necessary. But I insisted and went off payroll for the next two weeks, turning up on the job site to help solve the major problems. I didn't want to do this work unpaid, but I felt my reputation depended on leaving in the right way. The executives at Lathrop and their customers would know I was a man who completed what he started and took pride in his work.

I vividly remember the newspaper report announcing the formation of my new company, MacKinnon-Douglas, Inc.: "Mr. Douglas, a native of Bloomfield Hills, Mich., who spent three years with Entenman and the last three years with The Lathrop Company, both Toledo-based contractors, said that MacKinnon-Douglas will do general contracting in Michigan and Indiana and will not be in com-petition with the Toledo firms with which he has been associated."

It was 1964, and I was 30 years old.

For capital, I invested most of my savings, $15,000. Another $50,000 came as a loan from Hector MacKinnon, the president of Entenman, my first employer after I left the Navy and now my partner.

When an entrepreneur plans the start of a company, he often wants to offer a piece of it to strong businessmen around him. That's a mistake. All you can get from these people is advice, which is readily available, and you'll be saddled with partners who can tell you what to do. You create impediments, not impetus.

No matter how much expertise or talent a company has, it has to seek new business. To do that, you have to build trust with your potential customers. For a new company without a track record, that's a major challenge. I was keen not to compete with Entenman, so made a concerted effort to develop my own prospects, people, and projects, recalling the example of the president of Lathrop:

Almost every situation in life is a sales situation,
and selling will always be about relationships.
You seek to solve other people's problems.

Starting a business forces you back to first principles. There are no shortcuts. Self-discipline, hard work, and the building of trust are vital.

WORK HABITS OF AN ENTREPRENEUR

As an entrepreneur, the last thing you can be is a clock watcher. If anything, you must show up earlier, work later, plan better, and execute more effectively than the people you're working with and those you're competing against. For the first 25 years of running my own business, I did all of the structural engineering work. The rule at our house: Every night when I was in town and not traveling, we had dinner as a family, and after that, when everyone was in bed, I would clear the kitchen table, clamp on a drafting device, spread out my structural and foundation plans, and work until the early hours.

Even in those early days, I led by example. When I visited a site, I would never just drive up in midmorning and talk to my superintendent through the car window. I would arrive before he did and walk over the project, talking through the problems and figuring out how to solve them together.

But it's never easy, and **when you're starting out, others will take advantage of you. They know you're eager to prove yourself and that you must work to do that.** Even my partner MacKinnon did this.

One day, he came in and told me Entenman had won a contract to build a hospital building with a lift slab process, which meant you poured the floors onto the ground and jacked them into place up on steel columns. He said, "We've priced it and we think we can build this as a total concrete frame, cast in place, much less expensively, but the architect won't redesign it. The design engineer said we can do it if we redesign it ourselves. So would you redesign the building for us?" His was a separate company, and doing this work would take time from the effort of my new firm, in which he was an investor.

It involved a lot of effort, in addition to all I was doing to get the company off the ground, but I did it because he was my partner. And for just the same reason, he didn't feel it necessary to pay me the $60,000 engineering fee I would normally have charged.

Another challenge is finding good people to join you. Often, you just have to make do. It was not easy persuading the first few people to work with me, but once they had a good experience and word got out, a strong hire became a lot easier to find. The character of a company is set by the first ten people you hire.

When I had to hire my first project superintendent, I met a number of candidates before meeting a guy called Fred Kruse, who I wanted to oversee a shopping center 100 miles away from his home. The only problem was he didn't have a truck. I bought him one, and he ended up working for me until he retired.

JFK'S WHITE HOUSE

Hiring and staffing could follow the example of John Kennedy's White House. Walt Rostow, who advised Kennedy on national security, wrote that the president's organization:

"did not fit the hierarchical pyramids to be found in textbooks on administration: it was like the spokes of a wheel. When he formed a bond it remained firm. His enormous energy permitted him to deal with a great many people on a bilateral basis, weaving their efforts into his tasks as he saw them. His method was that of the extended family. . . . He put each member to work in ways that could help, according to his talents. It was rooted in an assessment of human beings that was both affectionate and hard-minded. He actively enjoyed the variety of talents and personalities that assembled around him as the drive for the presidency gathered momentum. He respected each man for what he was. There was reliability in his acceptance of men to work with him. There was also a firm assessment of where each might be useful."

Later in life, notably during my involvement in politics, I would approach something closer to the Kennedy White House ideal. But as a young entrepreneur, I did what I could with those I had.

For all my best efforts early in my career, there was still a lot I needed to learn on the job. I had never negotiated agreements, for instance, nor had to win contracts for my company. Now it was all up to me. Some people will tell you that when you are starting out, you have to pretend to be what you are not, or to fake it till you make it. I prefer to think of the challenge in terms of confidence, or honest arrogance. Architect Frank Lloyd Wright said that early in his career he had to choose between honest arrogance and hypocritical humility; naturally he took the honest course. **You have to know you can do the job and convey that confidence to a customer who naturally might be drawn to a more established rival.**

Ralph Lauren tells the story of his earliest days in business, when he was in his 20s, and had designed his own line of ties, wider than most ties then on the market. He struggled for weeks to get a meeting with the buyer at Bloomingdale's, then the most important department store in New York City.

When he managed to meet him, the buyer said: "Ralph, I like the patterns—but you have to make them a quarter of an inch narrower. And I want you to take your name off and put on Sutton East," the name of Bloomingdale's private label.

But Lauren held his ground. "Gary, I'm dying to sell to Bloomingdale's, but I'm closing my bag because I can't take my name off. And I can't make the tie a quarter of an inch narrower."

A few months later, after the ties had proved popular in other stores, Bloomingdale's was asking to sell them on Lauren's terms.

Starting your own business requires humility, a willingness to suck up your pride, but it also requires confidence in what you have to sell, even when a shortcut might seem an attractive answer.

Lauren has said that early on he faced severe financial struggles. He hired a friend to run the financial side of the business, but the friend was sloppy about paying bills, and very soon Lauren was in trouble. He was scared of losing everything, and even more, he was worried about disappointing his father, who had trusted and encouraged him to set up his own business. So Lauren put his last penny into the business and made it through. The immensely stylish and successful company we see today had the same scrappy, edgy growing pains as millions of other start-ups.

My father probably thought I was crazy to put it all on the line, but we were in different worlds. He was happy with what happened with the company, though he never said he was proud of me. Thus I never worried about disappointing him.

BUILDING TRUST AND BUSINESS

It is always easy to overcomplicate business with strategies and forecasts and the torrent of daily minutiae. But in those early days, when people asked what I did, I told them it was pretty simple. I went out and signed agreements with people to represent their interests by building on time and on budget with the highest quality and in such a way that we all made money. Do that enough times and customers start to trust you, and when they trust you, they give you their business.

To have a five year plan you must survive and prosper in the first 12 months, and then you can think long term.

Slowly, my business grew, with clients in Michigan and Ohio, and a broad range of projects, from shopping centers to schools, courthouses to manufacturing plants. At every turn, I tried to be innovative to solve problems for my customers. The Fulton Tubing company of Ohio, for example, once needed a clear span within a certain height restriction for its manufacturing process. The roof height of the factory was insufficient, so I came up with a prestressed steel truss of my own design that did the job.

But you can never take that trust for granted. Every year, Fulton needed another addition, and the company's engineers came and went. One would agree with our budget and the next would come in and think we were overcharging. I recall one engineer churlishly agreeing to pay the bills he inherited from his predecessor and saying he never wanted to see me again.

A month later he called to say, "I've got to build a parking lot, and I don't know who to call. I hate to call you—but at least I know who you are."

So I went to the site, calculated the grades, designed the parking lot and utilities for him, contracted with somebody to build it, and delivered drawings and bids to him. I told him I wouldn't charge him for anything I'd done since he seemed to feel entitled to the work anyway. We ended up building his parking lot, I supervised, and it was finished on time. After that, we continued adding onto that plant and later built another factory for the same engineer in southern Ohio.

One day the owners of Fulton Tubing, then part of ITT, asked me to go to Arkansas to look at an industrial park in Searcy, where they were having a groundbreaking for a new facility. On the dais, after the governor spoke, one of their guys said, "We're going to build this plant, and there's our contractor sitting right there."

He was pointing at me.

I had no idea what I was being signed up for, and they hadn't given me any details—but they knew from my previous work that our company could be trusted to deliver what it promised.

There were always opportunities to explore new ideas. The Gershensens of Detroit, one of our key clients, asked me to go to Portland, Oregon, to examine the status of the soil where they were to build a mall on an island in the Columbia River. The condition was called liquefaction, meaning that the soil would turn to soup if there was an earthquake.

I resisted going, but Richard Gershensen said, "Come on, we'll go out together and have a good time."

I designed a foundation system to deal with liquidity, and Richard convinced us to build the buildings.

Richard's father, Bill, was one of my mentors. When we were building a shopping center for him in Port Huron, Michigan, he said to me, "You're too concerned with the details and extra costs. Here's the deal: As we proceed, every time there's a change, write me a letter with a price. When we get to the end of the work we'll settle all those items."

That seemed a little strange, but I trusted him as he did me. At the end, he looked at this list of items and said some were his, some were mine, and some we should split. It all worked out fine.

Success, I've always believed, belongs to the problem solvers. Entrepreneurs can approach solutions through analysis and synthesis. Particularly, though, they rely on *insight*–suddenly and unexpectedly achieving a solution through a process that is not consciously reportable.

In any transaction, you can fight over details. But my way has always been to do what I think best for the client and let the chips fall where they may. Whether they end up paying or not, I'd rather act in their interests than against them.

Give people more than what they think they're entitled to,
and the future will take care of itself.

For instance, when there was a mistake in a building, or a failure to conform or perform, our policy was to fix it rather than argue. When the repair was done, it was easy to see who was culpable and we could go to that person and collect. Otherwise, there can be disputes and litigation, which would interfere with the relationship.

Over the years MacKinnon-Douglas merged with Entenman to form MacKinnon-Parker, Inc., which survived the death of MacKinnon and kept on growing. At that point, I owned stock in the company with three other partners: a carpenter (son-in-law of the founder), an accountant, and an engineer. They were accustomed to contracting as an adversarial business. They'd bid each job for a fixed price and then fight with the customer to do only what was specified and nothing more. They were often baffled by my more consensual, value-creating approach, and I should have bought them out. Instead we kept lurching along, arguing but still growing.

ADVOCATE, NOT ADVERSARY

I was constantly trying to instill the idea that we should be our customers' advocates rather than their adversaries. It was an uphill battle. I held seminars for all of our people and preached about the effect that becoming advocates would have on our lives and our income. I told them profit margins double when you negotiate contracts and invest in a continuing relationship. But, often, all I got were blank stares from my partners. I underestimated how entrenched people could be in their habits and functional roles. Many of them were only focused on doing their own job in a certain way, not caring about the future or any alternatives. Experts' mindsets were often the hardest to change.

When we founded the first company, there were still a few areas of expertise I hadn't mastered. I hadn't negotiated many contracts, and I'd never had to go out to find new customers.

But after six years, those gaps in my knowledge had been filled in. I had been fighting to change the company for what seemed like a long time, and I was tired of it.

During the most difficult times, my frustrations would manifest themselves physically. For the first time in my life, I would frequently find myself tired. I would lie down at lunchtime and again after dinner. When I could not move the company in the direction I wanted, I would feel worn out. Then a problem would be overcome, and I would briefly feel emancipated. Part of me wanted to stay in there and fight as an entrepreneur, but my feelings and my own body had another agenda.

In 1975, I let the other shareholders buy me out, left the company, and went skiing with my family in Colorado.

If you are trying to change a company with a staid vision to one with an entrepreneurial orientation, you must have both control and time. It's hard for those accustomed to "hard money" construction—which takes advantage of every opportunity in a "cost to the client" oriented business—to end adversity and add advocacy. The fact that all of the people who were in that business with me were successful didn't alter the difficulty of change; I was at a disadvantage because, contrary to Uncle Gilbert's advice, I had invested in a firm I could not control.

ALWAYS REMEMBER:

- Finding the right balance between work and family is crucial, and it's always a challenge.

- Almost every situation in life is a sales situation.

- You must under promise and over deliver for a bright future.

- You and the bank exist for each other; there must be reciprocal trust and care.

- An impediment is actually an opportunity and a problem you should want to solve.

- If you say you'll do it, get it done; there must be no compromise on small or large items.

- Solve the problems, protect the relationship and don't sweat the small stuff.

- Your company is the vehicle for providing employees with the means for their own fulfillment and you must genuinely display that.

- A carefully crafted plan with insights into your people will lead to success.

- Protect your downside for the upside will take care of itself.

- Cut your losses short and let your profits run.

- Life operates in reverse action to entropy; therefore the universe is hostile to life. Progress is a continual effort to swim against the stream

- Business is the highest evolution of consciousness, responsibility and morality.

- By adhering to a strong honest philosophy you will remain guiltless, blameless and independent while maintaining control of your life.

- The right thing is usually not the easy thing to do; thus you may sacrifice popularity for rightness, but you lose self-esteem for wrongness.

- Don't be afraid to say "No".

- Contributing to the learning of young people leads to exciting venues in education of which you can be part.

FOUR

PLAIN SAILING AND STRAIGHT TALKING

*"People will always try to stop you from doing
the right thing if it is unconventional."*
—Warren Buffett

It was my then-secretary, Maxine, who pulled me back into the construction business. Soon after I had left the old company, MacKinnon-Parker, she had been fired. She called me up in Vail and said: "Let's go back in the construction business. I have everything organized, and I know what to do. You just have to come back and do what you do."

My enthusiasm was tempered by my recent experience. I had made enough money by that point that I didn't have to go back to work. But I was still fascinated by engineering and construction. If I was to set up another company, it would have to be completely on my terms. **This time, I had to have complete control**. Control was why I'd wanted to be an entrepreneur in the first place. No more partners meddling and telling me what to do. No more complacency and bad habits. My personal life was settled, my financial position was sound, and I was ready to take another risk.

To finance my new venture, I took a note I owned for $600,000 for my former company's stock to my bank, The First National Bank of Toledo.

"I need money for this note," I said to the chairman, Chas McKelvey.

"Well, I'll take it to the board of directors," he said. "I don't know if that company will be able to pay off that debt without you."

"Don't take it to the board of directors," I said and left, angry at the chairman's doubt.

Another bank, Toledo Trust, had asked me a number of times to do business there. So I walked down the street and took the note to a vice president there, Don Breese. "I need money for this note. I'm going into business."

"Turn it over and sign it," he said. "The money will be in your account by the morning. You might have trouble collecting payment from your former stockholders, but we won't." That was a nice vote of confidence from the bank, and I never heard about that note again.

A healthy rather than acrimonious relationship with a bank
is vital for any entrepreneur.

I learned this from Dean Bailey, a good friend and real estate developer in Toledo. We were once working with another developer on a couple of shopping centers in Ohio. Before the developments had even started, I'd taken the developer to our bank to arrange a loan for one of the projects. But this developer went broke, and we had to take over the projects. I discovered later that he'd borrowed another $50,000, in addition to the $1.5 million I'd helped him secure. When the bank called it in, I told them: "That $50,000 isn't my problem. You lent him that separately."

Fortunately, Dean pulled me aside and said, "That *is* your problem. You introduced that deadbeat to the bank. You brought him in there. He's your responsibility. So you go to the bank and tell them you'll take the hit for that $50,000 loan."

I said, "I don't think that's right."

"You just don't get it," he said.

He took me to the bank, and I did tell them I had introduced the developer to them and that I would take care of the additional loan.

Dean's opinion was that banks have to make loans to guys like us, people who are going to pay them back. If they didn't make loans to good, dependable clients, then they wouldn't be in business and neither would we. We exist for each other, and preserving that trust involves sucking up the occasional $50,000 loan gone sour. Having a good reputation and friendly relationships with my local banks has served me well time and again during my career.

Starting a business the second time around was infinitely easier. People knew me and trusted me, and I was well capitalized. I also knew what I was doing. Very quickly, The Douglas Company had its first deal, a shopping center outside Pontiac, Michigan.

During our negotiations, the developer asked me about my organization.

"It's just Maxine and me," I told him.

"Why would I contract with somebody whose organization is just him and a secretary?" the developer asked.

"This is the best deal you ever had," I told him. "This is my first job in this new company, and if I fail, I'll be out of business."

He nodded, shook my hand, and we were off.

Maxine was right. All we had to do was do what we knew, and the business began to flow. Every night she would drop a briefcase at my home with checks to sign, contracts to finish, and decisions to be made. Each morning at dawn, I'd leave the completed work on her doorstep, then work with projects and clients.

This time around, hiring was easy. People wanted to work for us and believed we would grow and prosper. When we signed a lease on a building, we threw all our things in the back of our trucks and moved in one Saturday morning. We then went to our company bar, Shawn's Back Door, to celebrate.

Every organization needs a company bar, and Shawn's was laid out backwards because the owner thought that the best saloons he had been to were entered through the alley, thus the name. When you entered Shawn's, the first thing you saw was two doors, labeled "Men" and "Women."

Unfortunately, I forgot to pay the tab when we left; I just stuck the bill in my jeans and went home. The waitress showed up at our office on Monday morning to remind me of that and said she'd been fired. When I offered to help, she said, "No, I didn't like the manager anyway, that's fine."

Our biggest clients in those days were Kmart and Kroger, the supermarket chain. On a single day in 1976, we broke ground on five different shopping centers in Ohio and Michigan, each anchored by a Kroger store.

I tried to be innovative in every area of the business, from financing to construction. I built supermarkets financed by the bank, guaranteed by a promise of eventual payment from the customer. But above all, I made sure the job got done.

I solved other people's problems for them
and in that way built my business.

One of the biggest headaches when building Kroger supermarkets was the HVAC heating and cooling system, which had to be positioned inside the store. We essentially had to build the building around it. At one point, so many Kroger stores were being built in America that deliveries for these HVAC systems were backed up. One of my projects was facing a serious and expensive delay, and I was doing the construction financing.

So I called Typhoon, the maker of the units. They explained the problem was a shortage of the coils that lay at the heart of the system. A new supplier in Atlanta was testing more, but it was going to take time. I asked if they would build me a unit if I got my own coil.

They said yes, so I sent one of our employees, a big man with an eye-patch over one eye, down to Atlanta, where he rented a truck and showed up at the coil factory. He bought a coil and drove it all the way up to Cleveland, where they made the units. This was on Monday. By Thursday, after exerting more pressure on the manufacturer, I had my HVAC unit. My one-eyed truck driver drove it to Michigan;

we installed it in the supermarket and walled it in. Kroger's head of construction was furious, saying we had jumped the line and the unit was destined for another store. He yelled and screamed for a while, but eventually we both started laughing.

We had been desperate guys. Our slogan came from Winston Churchill: "In a guerilla operation, doing your best isn't enough. You have to do what's necessary." We had to get this done, and we had taken the initiative to do it—to get the coil when no one else would. That's what it took to get the job done, and that was a risk I was willing to take.

For a businessperson to try to get something moving along, you don't necessarily have to do what's best or what's expected. You have to do what's required. I'd done this to make money as a child and as an engineer in the Navy, and I never stopped as an entrepreneur.

Problems are opportunities in disguise, provided, of course, you do what you promise to do.

Entrepreneurs need to be creative and innovative, and they have to realize that what may look like an impediment is actually an opportunity, a challenge, and a problem they should want to solve. It's the Irish who always seem to be looking for adversity, and I respond to that. The effect on morale of doing what's seen as impossible is immense.

If anyone doubted me, I would say: "Look, if that isn't done by Monday as promised, then look in the obituaries, because I'll be dead, and that's where you'll find me. You won't find me here at the office." **If I say I'll get it done, I'll get it done.** When customers know this, they trust you with their toughest problems.

On one occasion, we started a shopping center outside Cleveland for a developer, and the excavating company we hired pulled out. They considered the soil too unstable and the job too hard.

We had delivered a bond to guarantee we would finish the job.

And a promise is a promise, so we rented equipment and did the earthwork ourselves. We understood the problem and the soil situation, and even though the workload was daunting, we knew how to do it. Our guys on the project were exceptionally good at understanding those situations, and we had good soil engineers we could call on as consultants when we had a problem. We came through and had the satisfaction of solving a very difficult problem.

Solving hard problems not only pleases the customer, it also makes you a better company. It forces you to get better at everything, to become more efficient, more creative, and, ultimately, more profitable. It was Samuel Johnson who said, "Knowing you're to die at dawn concentrates the mind wonderfully."

We became experts in materials and construction techniques because we never sought the easy way out. Many companies can do the simple jobs, but that is not the way to make money or build confidence with your clients. We were always trying to do more and do it better than ever before.

The head of construction at Kroger once challenged us to build a store in 21 weeks. We decided to go one better and covered our five construction sites with huge signs, each the size of a house, which said "20," and under that "The Douglas Company." The Kroger team came out and asked what it meant. It meant we could build a store in 20 weeks, which soon became 19, then 18.

Many construction companies typically bid jobs too cheaply and then figure they will make the money back when bargaining with subcontractors. We never did that. **We were rarely the cheapest, but people kept hiring us because we delivered.**

We focused on creating value for our customers by promising three things: on-time completion, cost control, and quality. Do those three, and do them right, and the money follows.

We went into each project knowing what we had to do, whom we had to deal with, and what was expected of us. Many people would say to us, "Kmart representatives are very hard to deal with— too strict and too interested in crossing t's and dotting i's."

And to this I replied: "We just give them exactly what they ask for. They're very clear about what they want."

That works, and it turns out to be rather simple.

I also had a policy of always charging our clients enough that we didn't have to sweat the small stuff. If a client wanted a specific change made, even though he wasn't entitled to it, we could just do it; we didn't have to haggle over every last cent. Of course, we'd remind the clients we weren't supposed to perform such tasks, but in the end, we'd aim to please them and not argue about it. That's true of problems at the end of the work as well. If you argue about the difficulty and try to find who is culpable, there is acrimony and delay. Remember, if you fix what is wrong, it is easy to find out who is at fault, and then you can go ahead and ask for payment from the appropriate party. They almost always pay, whether architect, sub-contractor, or owner.

HOW TO SETTLE A
DISPUTE WITH A CLIENT

We were once building a nursing home in Las Vegas, and the people in our Orlando office disagreed with the owner over some extra costs and delay expenses. I went to see the client and said, "We have a bunch of items here that we have to resolve."

He responded, "Here's what we'll do: You and I will be an arbitration panel and our guys and your guys will come in and present their ideas and concepts, and then you and I will decide."

My men, who created the situation, thought I was nuts to agree. But I thought it was worth taking the chance, and we listened to all the pros and cons of each issue, sat down together, reviewed all of the options, and resolved it. The final payment by the owner exceeded what our people expected.

That's the way disputes with clients should be settled.

Mutual trust and confidence produces good discussion
and plenty of options. You can have disagreements,
but you can work through it.

My construction manager, Wally Miller, had served as a warrant officer in the Marine Corps and believed in straight talk and keeping promises, however difficult that may be. Wally, five foot three, 140 pounds, showed up in my office early in the company's history and said he could build the high rise apartment we were scheduled to construct in Detroit, a tough place to work. He also said he was an alcoholic.

I remember going with Wally to discuss problems with a client concerning a shopping center in North Carolina we had managed poorly. He told the developer how we would correct the situation.

The developer looked over at me. "I want to know what the boss thinks."

But Wally interjected: "You don't understand. **The job's the boss**. We're going to do what's right for the job, and I just told you what that is. That's what we're going to do."

I never said a word.

Years later, we had made such a mess of a project in South Carolina that I got in the car to drive to the job site with Wally, vowing to fire everybody there.

Wally changed my mind. "We're going to support our people," he said. "That's what great companies do, and we're a great company. We're going to go up there and fix it, and we're going to support our people in the process."

He was right. **I'm grateful I had someone who could say to me, "You're on the wrong track," and say it loudly enough for me to listen**. Unfortunately, I can recall times when I haven't listened. If I had, I would have saved myself considerable difficulty and grief. Wally helped teach me the importance of respect for people's feelings and their situation and to listen to them with respect.

YOUR ROLE AS LEADER

Entrepreneurs are often such driven people they forget that not everyone is like them. Your role as the leader of a company is not just to lead but also to serve the people who work for you. It is to help them be better, to learn more, to grow and earn. Your relationship with someone who works for you is like a bank account. Each time you help them or give them ways to enhance themselves, you're making a deposit. But if you go in and say, "Shut up and do this my way by Friday," you're making a withdrawal. Too many withdrawals and you're bankrupt.

This, I learned later at Sterling College, is servant leadership. We teach it and live by it.

If I can make somebody's life better, improve their situation, and make it easier for them to learn and grow, then I'm really serving them. Whether or not that's ultimately self-serving doesn't matter. When I was running MacKinnon-Parker, I was spending some of what I had made building a house in the best part of town.

I asked my assistant, "Does anybody care that I'm building an expensive home?"

She said nobody cared.

You're entitled to do what you want to do. But if you pound your chest and say, "Let me show you the pictures of my big, new house," you will get hurt.

Your company is a vehicle for providing employees with a means for their own fulfillment. If you're not genuine about it, it'll kill you. I found that people got a lot of satisfaction from their jobs while working for me, and they made more money than they ever could have made anywhere else. I would put an amount equal to 15% of their salary every year into a profit-sharing plan, and if I couldn't do that, they should have gotten rid of me. **If you are standing beside the hospital bed of someone who is dying who has worked for you, and if there is not enough money for his wife to carry on and live a good life, you have failed.** That does not make you a good person. That is your responsibility. Most people do not save money; you have to help them.

I don't think people think about sticking with a single organization. The grass is always greener. But if you set things up correctly, they will stay. I remember hiring an older Polish superintendent named Zigmond Gawron, who came to me one day and said one of my project managers was stealing from me. It was a strange emotional experience.

This project manager was a big guy, six foot six, 250 pounds. I sat down with my team and figured out what to do: I'd let him finish the projects he was involved in and fire him on a Friday afternoon. It was a calm process. Then, as I started down the corridor that day and got into the project manager's office, I wanted to grab him by the scruff of the neck and throw him out on the street. It was very emotional.

Eight months later, the he came to me and asked for his job back.

First I said, "Tell me you did it."

He did.

I asked others around the office: "Should I hire him back?"

They all said, "Yes, he's useful."

I asked Zig, who said, "Yes, take him back, on one condition." Zig didn't want to work with him.

I took the man back, and he worked for me for ten more years.

A while later, Zig got behind schedule and ran into some problems on a job. We had breakfast in a little deli in Orlando, and we talked about the mistakes he'd made. He said at the end of the breakfast, "You sonofabitch, I'm going to work for you until the day I die."

There is no HR policy for this type of situation—but people will support you if you give them a chance, if you understand that we are all human and worthy of support.

ALWAYS REMEMBER:

- There will be times in your life when dramatic change is possible; cusps which allow you to focus on opportunities and people. Cherish these times as key chances to learn and grow.

Bruce's grandmother, Margaretta Biddle
Douglas, of the famous Biddle family in
Philadelphia.

Bruce and his grandfather,
Thomas Cosgrove.

Benjamin Douglas, Bruce's
father and Kathleen
Cosgrove, Bruce's mother.

Bruce and his
sisters, Jean, left,
and Kathie.

Bruce as a youngster.

Bruce and Dee with their
son, Peter, in Port Heuneme,
California where Bruce was in
the Civil Engineering Corps'
Officers' School.

Bruce, back row, third from left, in 1956, with his staff in Japan.

Dee, in 1960, doing an ad for a washer and dryer.

The Douglas family celebrating Christmas in 1963.

The Douglas children, Anne, Susan and Peter, visiting a construction site. Bruce took them to a construction site every Saturday.

Sterling College President Dr. Bruce Douglas, second from left, with Kansas Governor Kathleen Sebelius, Congressional Medal of Honor winner, Paul Bucha, and Sterling College Trustee Darryl Ness.

Sterling College President Dr. Bruce Douglas with his sister, Jean, at a Sterling College Commencement.

Sterling College President Dr. Bruce Douglas, dressed as a bug, visits with a student in one of the new dormitories on campus. A soccer student who complained about bugs in the dormitory prior to landscaping being done around the buildings invited the president to spend the night in the dorm. Dr. Douglas dressed as a bug, took a half-a-dozen pizzas to the dorm at 11 p.m. and stayed up until 3 a.m. talking with students. The soccer student then told Dr. Douglas, "There's your bunk over there." That's where Dr. Douglas slept that night.

The cover of Sterling College magazine's Winter 2006 edition featured President Dr. Bruce Douglas visiting with students. An article in the magazine detailed his background and how he came to be the school's president in the fall of 2005. He led the college for more than three years.

The Next Development

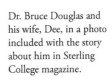

Dr. Bruce Douglas and his wife, Dee, in a photo included with the story about him in Sterling College magazine.

Nicolas Biddle, President of the Second Bank of the United States, who is an ancestor of Bruce Douglas. Nicolas Biddle was also the subject of Bruce's Ph.D. dissertation.

I am very respectfully / Yours,

Bruce Douglas, far left, with members of the Douglas Company Board of Directors at their retirement when the company was sold in 2000.

Celebrate 2000

Dr. Bruce Douglas, President of Sterling College, with Rigoberto Medina at graduation.

Dr. Bruce Douglas, left, with Dr. John Silber, President Emeritus of Boston University, at an honors ceremony at the University of Toledo. Dr. Silber was the commence-ment speaker at Sterling College in 2008.

Bruce Douglas, rowing on the Maumee River in Toledo, Ohio.

Dr. Bruce Douglas

Plaza Apartments in Toledo, Ohio. In 1982, The Douglas Company bought this old residential hotel located near the Art Museum. One of the buildings, which had been destroyed by fire, had to be rebuilt. Peter Douglas, just out of graduate school with an MBA, was the superintendent for this project, which has since been remodeled and updated, and donated to the Catholic Diocese of Toledo.

In 1985, The Douglas Company and partners who were directors of Health Care REIT, a public real estate investment trust, used expensive REIT financing and syndicated equity to build the West Park Place Apartments, a senior housing and assisted living community in Toledo, Ohio. The project was easy to build, but difficult to lease. Eventually, West Park Place was sold to another investor.

In 1987, The Douglas Company built the Orient Prison in Orient, Ohio. The $60 million project was completed on time and within budget.

Uptown Arts Apartments in Toledo, Ohio. This urban redevelopment project by Harvard Development Company included 52 apartments with artists' lofts and gallery space. Tenants moved into the units of this subsidized affordable housing development in 2002.

New Cheney Flats, a subsidized affordable housing development built by Harvard Development Company in 2002, included 65 apartments and townhouses with 40-foot-deep retail and gallery spaces along Adams Street in downtown Toledo, Ohio.

FIVE

TAKING RISKS

*"A very great deal more truth can become
known than can be proven."*
—Richard Feynman, Nobel Laureate, 1965

Entrepreneurs are generally assumed to be risk-takers. But in my experience, they are more managers of risk than takers of it.

I often think the greatest risk I could have taken would have been not to pursue my dream of building and running my own business. It would have been far more dangerous for me to accept a life of quiet desperation and unfulfilled ambition than to do what I have done.

The way an entrepreneur controls risk is through careful analysis, hard work, and sound management. I recommend to you a book entitled *What Color Is Your Parachute?* It's essentially a working process in which you look at skills, values, and favorite environment. For me, the study involved three hours every Saturday morning one summer at the lake. The result is a summary that deals with salary, philosophy of life, tasks, outcomes, skills, people, and tools. You end up with a series of conclusions arranged in what they call "petals." These can guide your life. An example is in the appendix.

On the first day of each year, I go to a quiet place and write a list of the things I plan to do that year. Then, every Saturday morning, I sit on the dock by the lake with my notes and analyze what I did that week—emphasizing public esteem, impact, passion, elegance, important tasks, important people, and status. Then I write out a plan for the oncoming week, and I think about it for a while.

It's amazing what happens in that process.

One hour of precise, integrated thinking can be worth
a month of hard work.

It's easy in business and in life to be yanked around by the most immediate and pressing problems. But if you do not act beyond your feelings, and instead follow the path of least resistance, you're giving in to laziness and can no longer control your life. That's the much bigger risk.

Identifying exactly what it is you want takes a lot of thought. But if you start with the end in mind, invest in that and prepare for it, and visualize yourself getting what you want, you at least have a shot. I learned from my father, the socialist, that the best way to accomplish your business goals is by making service to others your primary goal. Your success will come from adding value to other people's lives. If your purpose in life is personal security, you will be a failure.

Nonetheless, there will always be moments of great stress if you pursue the entrepreneurial path, those nights when you stare at the ceiling wondering what on earth you have gotten yourself into.

Sometimes, all you need to do is adjust your perspective.

I remember once undertaking a mixed-use development in downtown Toledo and having it rejected by the planning commission. That night, I could not sleep, and Dee asked me what was bothering me. I told her the commission had turned down my plan, and the only recourse was a lawsuit.

"What do you have invested in it?" she asked, as cool and rational as ever.

"About $400,000. But you know, I could write off that money and be okay in the morning."

I went back to sleep.

I was all caught up in the defeat and Dee asked exactly the right question to put my mind at rest. If I'd had $20 million I had to write off, I'd probably have felt differently about it. But this was a level of risk I had consciously decided to assume going in. And, in any case, the very next morning, an official with the planning commission called to explain how we could modify our plans to have them approved. We did, we built the development, and everything worked out fine. I need not have lost a moment's sleep.

But then, I'm not a swing-for-the-fences kind of guy. **I'm not going to risk it all and put everything on the line.** There are people who are motivated by that sort of risk and danger, but I'm not one of them.

Sam Walton borrowed from his father-in-law to open his first store, and once he'd cleared his debts and paid off his house, borrowed again and again to build up his chain of Wal-Marts. He finally cleared his debts with an initial public offering. But his borrowing for his business was offset by his frugal personal habits: living in the same modest house, driving a pickup truck, and behaving very differently from most men of his means.

Richard Branson says that on several occasions in his career he decided to bet everything on an opportunity. "In my speeches, I will always say you have to protect the downside. But there have been occasions when I have asked my wife to sign a bit of paper. And she would say, 'What's that, dear?' And I would always say, 'Don't worry,' when it was actually the third mortgage on the house. But I really do believe that if something is important enough you should go and bet the damn house."

I know of one real-estate developer who is motivated by always being near bankruptcy. On Monday morning he'd be near default on loans, and he'd have to figure out a way to save himself from going over the brink. But I'm not a wild gambler like that. I prefer to take my risks in solving difficult engineering problems rather than fending off the banks.

NO SURPRISES

When I do confront a risky situation, I do so methodically. I take Ben Franklin's approach and list the pluses and minuses side by side. I do a lot of planning and analysis on my own every week, analyzing where I am, what I have, why, what the opportunities are, and what the risks are, so I am rarely surprised.

Bill Walsh, the Hall of Fame football manager, inherited a consistently losing team when he signed up to manage the San Francisco 49ers. He developed a long-term plan and linked it to a set of day-to-day actions, the secret of entrepreneurial success. He improved the infrastructure by hiring the right players and coaches to implement his West Coast offense and then drew up a three-year plan to get everything right.

He planned for the entire season, not just the next game, starting with pacing training and schedules and understanding opponents. He then meticulously designed a worksheet for each game, refusing to deviate under the pressure of events. He also took into account the possibility of various contingencies, expecting the unexpected. He would script the first 30 offensive plays of each game and memorize them; he knew that if he just winged it, he'd become predictable, and he intended to be unpredictable.

Then he made a sixth-round draft choice for his starting quarterback: Joe Montana from Notre Dame. Montana was skinny with a weak arm, but Walsh had spotted a competitive intelligence in him that would serve his system well. Walsh would happily trade great players if they didn't fit into his tightly meshed West Coast system. Four Super Bowl victories, the fourth a year after he retired, and many 49er players in the Hall of Fame are testament to the success of Walsh's methods.

Combining a carefully crafted plan with insights into your people leads to success.

We all ultimately make decisions with our hearts, but I've found, like Bill Walsh, that **if I do enough analysis, I tend to have the right information in my head *and* my heart can make the choice.**

For example, technical changes are as inevitable in construction as they are in many other businesses. You can either complain or adapt. My company was helped greatly by changes in the design codes for steel and concrete buildings and our readiness to make the best of these changes.

When I was in engineering school, designing concrete structures, the professor said, "A plane before bending is a plane after bending, and stress is proportional to strain. Don't ever forget that." At the time, it was the basic design concept upon which formulas were created. But, years later, it turned out not to be true, since concrete is strong in compression and weak in tension—which explains why we use reinforcing bars. After extensive testing, the formulas were changed to use load factors and empirically determined coefficients that made buildings more economical and sensible.

In steel structures, it was determined that when continuous beams and frames reached their yield stress, they didn't fail. Rather, the bending moments redistributed to other parts of the structure. Our buildings were designed with this new code, and we were able to build well at lower costs using those techniques.

I have always admired those able to take the complex and explain it in simple terms. The Nobel Prize winning physicist Richard Feynman had the rare gift of being able to express himself in ways the average person could understand. His mind operated in the highest realms of math and physics, but he could tie it all back down to practical problems, making it meaningful to people not as smart or well educated as he was. He became known to a large audience for his investigation into the causes of the Challenger space shuttle disaster. He was astonished to find the gulf between NASA's executives and its engineers, and management's desire to believe in outlandish estimates of the shuttle's reliability. He famously demonstrated the flaws in the shuttle's O-ring seals, which contributed to the disaster, by placing them in a cup of ice-cold water in a meeting and showing they lost their elasticity for a period afterward. With this simple experiment he showed what numerous graphs and equations could not have.

Feynman knew he could picture an answer to a question in physics, then proceed to prove the truth of his conclusion. His proofs were never absolute. He felt deciding on the answer is not scientific, and that to make progress one must leave the door to the unknown ajar—but only ajar. An American, Feynman admired the English for "muddling through" and not providing absolute answers so they wouldn't be chained to the limits of man's present imagination.

Government should not have the power to decide the validity of scientific theories, various descriptions of history, or economic theory or philosophy. Nothing should impede the ultimate development of the future human race. In that same way, the opportunities for the entrepreneur to explore possibilities and ambiguities are left open. In considering a problem, a scientist moves from ignorance, to uncertainty, to a feeling about the result that still contains doubt, and an entrepreneur treads the same path in search of knowledge and progress.

Much as I wished I possessed Feynman's powers of explanation, it was often left to me to use other methods to persuade engineers to accept my ideas. In the case of the continuous steel beams and concrete structures, I told them, "You have two choices: We'll build it the way it's designed, which will be more expensive, or we'll design it our way and be responsible for it— which will result in a savings— but we won't try to explain it to you."

That worked. I couldn't take an engineer back to school and teach him the new design methods, but I could take the responsibility and get the job done.

Foremost, regardless of the obstacles entrepreneurs–and engineers–encounter, they should absolutely do what they said they were going to do and never falsify. Lying is fatal.

I know of a building in Manhattan designed by a structural engineer who taught at Princeton and explained his design to his students after it had been built. The students told him he had designed the building with certain wind angles in mind but not others. He went back to his office, analyzed it, and observed that if the bracing was welded properly, there shouldn't be a problem. He went to the builder, who told him he had used bolted connections, not welds. With the students' critique nagging at him, he reanalyzed his calculations and drawings, and, to think it out, went to his summer home in New Hampshire with the printouts.

First, he told me, he wanted to kill himself. He realized he had made a huge mistake and repairing it would cost millions. But then he started thinking about solutions. He went back to the owner and recommended they put "Band-Aids" on all the bracing. They managed to get the patching done even as a hurricane approached the city. Imagine how this fellow felt when strain gauges were hooked up to his building during the repair and the hurricane was approaching.

After the storm had passed and the building had held up, the engineer went to the owners, who told him it had cost them $8 million to make the repairs. Architects and engineers have errors and omissions insurance, but he had only a million dollars' worth.

The owners said, "We'll take your million and pay the rest, and by the way, we think you're a hero for the way you handled this."

If the engineer had not had the courage to bring attention to his error, the consequences could have been far worse and might have cost lives.

Adversity is inevitable in every life and enterprise.
What is controllable is your reaction to it.

One of the toughest situations I ever found myself in was in the early 1980s. I had been doing business with a fine fellow named Joe Slavik, building apartments in Ann Arbor, Michigan.

He told me, "After we finish, you must go to downtown Detroit and build this project on the river."

I didn't really want to do that. I was afraid of building in Detroit because of the unions. But he insisted. So we did. **I should have trusted my instincts.**

He had a lawyer partner who turned out to be corrupt. Slavik died, and we had a terrible time completing the project. The lawyer had contracted with an inept architect and was unwilling to pay for changes that had to be made in the design. He siphoned off money that was intended for construction, and the whole project ended in a lawsuit, the only serious one I ever faced.

I sat in a courtroom in Detroit four days a week for four months. Imagine trying to run a business and being in that position. It went to the jury on a Thursday. We thought he owed us a million dollars, while he thought we owed him closer to $7 million. On Monday, I heard that the foreman of the jury had asked if they could give the lawyer/plaintiff more than he had requested.

Early the next morning, I sat down and said to myself, "Suppose I have to give the guy 10 million bucks. Where can I get the money in a way that doesn't affect the company or my family?" I wrote the numbers on a little piece of paper. "This is where 10 million comes from," and put it in a desk drawer.

I said to my secretary, "I'm going downtown to work for the kids in the inner city." At the time, Dee and I were putting a class of disadvantaged students through school. "I won't be back until about 4:30. Don't call me."

I got in the car, and I had this wonderful epiphany: "Nobody can hurt me. I can survive this or anything."

That's not true, of course, but that's the way it felt that morning.

I came back at 4:30, and my secretary hugged me. "We won. They owe us a million dollars."

It turned out the information I had heard on Monday about the foreman was wrong.

But what I remember most was the feeling I had while driving from our office outside Toledo to the downtown area where the kids were. It was wonderful. They found in London during the Blitz that the people who were not injured felt the same way. They had missed the damage and believed they were invincible. Perhaps it was surmounting an obstacle and knowing there was simplicity on the other side of chaos. Or the fact that I felt untouchable. It was what I had wanted all my life: to be in control of my own fate. And there I was faced with a lawsuit that might have sunk another man or another company, and I knew I could handle the worst of it.

I had clearly made a mistake getting involved in the Detroit project. I assigned too much importance to my relationship with Joe Slavik and succumbed to my pride rather than my reason or instincts. The client had asked me to trust that he would treat us fairly and meet us at least halfway, and I thought that agreement would neutralize any problems—but that wasn't how it turned out.

In retrospect, I mismanaged the risk. I didn't listen enough before deciding to get into the project. My project manager had looked at the deal and told me to drop it, as did others at my company. But I ignored them and listened instead to those who told me to do it for the good of the relationship and the difficulty of the challenge. They appealed to my vanity, my desire to be known as a problem solver, and they convinced me. I even ignored my own inner voice, which was telling me it was not the right deal, and I paid the price.

A couple of times I quit on the contract before I signed it, and the lawyer and Slavik's man came back and said, "We can't do this without you. You've got to do this deal." So I kept on going, but that was not a smart move.

I thought I was a great risk manager, ably balancing my natural conservatism with my desire to take on new and challenging projects. But this time, my judgment misfired. I failed to quantify the risks properly or listen to my people.

And I learned then–I hope for the last time–that it's much easier to get into a deal than to get out of one.

Having your personal life in good order is also vital to succeeding as an entrepreneur. My wife still complains about the number of hours I worked and the time I was away. But I think I did a pretty good job with that. After 59 years, we're still married—and our three kids are successful and don't complain.

KEEPING GROUNDED IS IMPORTANT

Ralph Lauren once explained that having a grounded family life was essential to his professional success and yet crucially separate from it. "We've always had the right value system about what's important in terms of family and people," he said. "That has nothing to do with being rich or poor. I could have less and essentially be the same person. Having success at an early age gave me more of a sense of what's important in life rather than always driving to make it. I loved what I did, and my satisfaction came from my own sense of stretching. I was fulfilled inside as opposed to needing outside fulfillment. Now, did I want good things that I'd never had? Yes. Did I have dreams about living this kind of life? Sure. Most everyone has those dreams—a nice house, a pool. That's part of the American thrust. Did I give up my family in order to have it? No. Did I jump to another group because they were going to make me bigger? Never. I have always been who I am."

For a lot of entrepreneurs, a big part of their success comes down to their spouse being there, running the household and taking care of the kids. That's certainly true of me, the entrepreneur. Dee says I only changed one diaper in my whole life. I've really been blessed because I married a woman who is a great wife and mother to our children. If our son and daughters hadn't turned out to be happy, successful adults, nothing else would have mattered. My life as a husband and father has been a wonderful experience and continues to be.

As a successful business person, you'll be approached from time to time by others who seek to hook up with you. Avoid them; they have agendas that are inimical to yours. Paul Newman had the best response when asked why he wasn't attracted to the beautiful women in his movies. Newman said of Joanne Woodward, "If you have steak at home, why would you go out for hamburger?"

My own family, my wife and children, also gave me a rock solid foundation as my own parents grew older. Interestingly, as I became successful, my father, the socialist who eschewed making money, responded positively to my financial situation. He enjoyed dinners, trips, and gifts that came his way because of my achievements. We still found it almost impossible to communicate. He said the only time we could talk was when we were in a car at night so we couldn't see each other and could speak freely.

What was going on here, this see-sawing between support and aloofness? **The good thing about his lack of support was that it forced me to rely on myself.** The only way I could go to college was by working various jobs and paying for it myself. There was an emphasis on academic excellence in our household, and we were expected to shine in school. Yet when selecting a college, my father gave me no support or advice. I suppose that was because I was paying for it and should make my own decision. Or perhaps it mirrored a vintner's philosophy when growing grapes for their wine: They believe that the vines must be stressed to produce the best grapes. This means they should be in a rock formation and stretch to reach the water in order to improve the quality of the product. Perhaps that was what my father was thinking, or maybe he just didn't care.

I had a radically different emotional experience at the passing of my mother than my father.

My sister Kathie called me one day in the midst of a big project development meeting to say our mother was in the hospital in Detroit. I went back to work with my people for an hour, and Kathie called again to say Mother had died. I told our engineers and administrators to come back in an hour to reconvene and finish the work—but 60 minutes later I was still crying and could not stop.

My mother was indomitable, and her loss was huge. She was critical, corrective but always supportive, and made me believe I could do anything I wanted to with my life.

When my father died, I remember no emotion whatsoever. He had been ill for about six months, the aftereffects of a second stroke, and I had done a lot to sustain him over that period. No tears, though, when he finally passed away. My father was not actively involved in my life in any meaningful way. His indifference to my general welfare and future prospects kept my feelings from surfacing—or even developing.

Starting my second company was undoubtedly much easier than starting my first. I knew more, and I had earned the trust of many more people. Banks knew me, employees knew me, developers knew me. I no longer had to prove myself before I could hire people, borrow capital, or get contracts. But there were also fresh challenges and risks, problems of hubris and over-reach, and always the challenge of learning to become a better entrepreneur and manager myself.

When you know so much about your own business, there's a strong temptation to micromanage. You think you're helping, but in fact what you are doing is misdirecting your own focus and showing a lack of trust in others.

Some people feel compelled to micromanage and have found success in using this technique with certain employees. But I do not think it is the most effective method; people perform better if they think for themselves and execute their own plan within the confines of the institution's mission. These are some of the ablest individuals, and you must keep them. We adopted the policy that the person in the location where the choice had to be made should make the decision, and we would not second-guess him.

I do not think you can have maximum success if you micromanage. You have to give people the opportunity to take the initiative, let people do their best and hardest work, and have confidence in them. It is important to have the right people in the right places and not to be afraid to replace them if they are not effective. You must understand the person's capabilities and limitations. This is how you create trust and feelings of self-sufficiency and competence in employees, which provide the bedrock of professional happiness. It is also how you learn.

Delegation and stepping back are perhaps the most vital skills in motivation.

It tells your employees you believe in them. Work itself is motivating. And praising someone is good. But even better is to show you believe in their talents. We had a site engineer who would be stuck on a problem and say it could not be solved in the available time. I would go into the engineering department early and sit at a drafting board, analyzing the problem, making notes and sketching. When the engineer came in he would come up to me, ask what I was doing, and we would talk about the possible results.

At that point, he would usually say to me, "Stand aside, I think I can solve this problem."

I would leave, and he would work it out. He would come back to me and show me his solution. I would give praise and approbation to the man for doing that. You have to acknowledge in front of everybody else that somebody did something special.

Money is a great motivator, but it is essential that employees feel your appreciation for them. Knowing you are part of a team that is getting something done and knowing that you did something that somebody else could not do, is very important.

If you are an entrepreneur, especially a serial entrepreneur, you may not necessarily be suited to run a company. As the founder or creator, you have to be willing to step back, observe what your strengths are, and know when *not* to be involved in managing.

Sometimes that truth hits an entrepreneur right between the eyes.

Once, when we were constructing a building for a company that was founded and being run by an entrepreneur, he said, "I was in a meeting when my associates came in and wanted to know what color to make the stripes in the parking lot. It hit me: If they're asking me questions like that, I'm too involved in running this."

Then it hit *me:*

I was planning to go to China for five weeks when I owned the Douglas Company. At that time, I was signing all the purchase orders, change orders and all the contracts, every check, and essentially looking at all the day-to-day operations. I told my colleagues I was going to China, I would be out of touch for weeks, and that I wasn't sure how they were going to take care of the five deals we had in the works, or how they would be able to complete all the tasks that existed.

The chief financial officer said, "We have a plan for that. You just never listened to us on how we can do this."

In those circumstances, you get back to the lowest common denominator with the right checks and balances.

I was gone for five weeks without communication, landed in San Francisco and called in to ask about my deals. They had made all five projects work.

I thought, "Gee, I should get back on the plane and go west. They don't need me."

It was a great feeling.

People who are in your organization generally know how it can be improved. Your job is to get them to tell you and then to act upon their suggestions.

ALWAYS REMEMBER:

- Have a sound plan, a strong honest philosophy and you will remain guiltless, blameless and independent while maintaining control of your life. Trust yourself and those around you and remember that the decision should be made by the person closest to the action, with complete support from all.

SIX

RECOGNIZE YOUR OWN LUCK

There used to be a construction firm in Monroe, Michigan, that did all the building work for a company called Foodtown. I wanted to build for Foodtown, too, so I went to its chief executive and asked, "Why do you keep hiring that other company?"

The CEO told me that several years before, the head of the other construction firm had gone broke, owing people a lot of money. Rather than curling up or disappearing, he had gone down to Florida, earned back the money, paid everyone off, and then come home. "And that's why we go with that guy," the man said.

There is a lot of forgiveness in the United States for this sort of thing. Perhaps more than there should be sometimes, but it is a great thing that we tolerate entrepreneurs failing and starting over.

During my business life, I had worked hard and been fortunate to find success. But I also believed strongly in stepping out of my comfort zone, of setting myself new challenges. You can never succeed, I believe, unless you risk failure. What I have found time and again is that once you take that step and become involved in something, it is not nearly as hard to be effective as you might have anticipated. In each commencement address, I tell graduates to expect failure. It goes with learning to succeed. **For an entrepreneur, challenges are what life is all about.**

THERE'S NO SUCCESS LIKE FAILURE

A friend, the great New York developer Sam LeFrak, and his wife Ethel used to have this wonderful old routine, which went like this:

Ethel: "Sam, how come you're so successful?"

Sam: "Good decisions."

Ethel: "Where did you get the good decisions?"

Sam: "Experience."

Ethel: "Where did you get the experience?"

Sam: "Bad decisions."

I could not agree more.

I never much liked, respected, nor sought to emulate my father, but he did leave me with a basic, liberal philosophy that all people have a right to be here and a need to assert their own ideas and concepts. Pop always insisted on civility, even to people I did not like. And from this belief stemmed his concern for fairness and honesty in the world. He really wanted to help people who were less fortunate but not in the classical, liberal sense of giving them money. He thought it was very important to provide opportunities. To him, education was the key, as was the opportunity for people to take advantage of schooling to learn and prosper. I always resented him for not taking more care over my education, though I guess I inherited his belief in the importance of it for others.

So in 1992, I decided to do something about it. I selected a group of children in the inner city of Toledo and told them I would help them. My goal was to support them from the time they were in elementary school through college, and ultimately to pay for their college education. It was not an original idea. Others had done it, yet it was something I wanted to do, and felt I should.

Dee was less than enthusiastic. She thought it was a dumb idea, a good way to waste a million dollars or more and not have much to show for it in the end; she did not believe most of them would get through college.

I nonetheless forged ahead.

We formed the Douglas Partnership 2000, named for the year the students would enter college, and set out to select 30 students in a third-grade inner-city class. When I showed the Toledo superintendent of the schools my plan, I expected an enthusiastic reception.

Unfortunately, I met immediate resistance.

"This causes problems for me," said the superintendent. "Have you thought about the research aspects of this?"

"No. I'm not interested in research," I told him. "I just want 30 kids. We'll support them, look after them, and, in effect, bring them into our family."

"What about the public relations part of this?" he asked.

"I don't think about that. I'm not doing this for public relations."

"You can't take one class in a school. You have to take two classes or it will be discrimination," he said.

"I don't want 60 kids. I can't handle 60 kids."

"You're causing problems for me."

"No, I'm not. I'm not causing problems," I said. "Let's just forget about it."

I then called the Catholic bishop of Toledo from my car and told him of my plan.

"What time do you go to work in the morning?" he asked.

"At seven o'clock."

"Can I bring a few others and meet you in your office?"

When we sat down together, I told him I wanted to help the toughest kids in the toughest school. I had no other criteria as to the level of learning or the social and economic demographics.

Instead of third graders, we selected a fourth-grade class with 30 students. It was a racially heterogeneous group—Hispanic kids, black kids, and white kids—and all were disadvantaged.

We then had a vice president at the University of Toledo write a formal plan. We drew up contracts with the parents and children stating the parents would support the students. It was the task of each student to study, concentrate, and work hard. Beyond that, they were not required to do anything except attend class and graduate high school, at which point their college education would be free.

The reaction from the children was great. At that age, they are very enthusiastic, and when I asked them what they wanted to do and what they wanted to be, they all had great hopes and high aspirations. They were very excited about their lives and futures. Even in fourth grade they understood what a free college education meant.

One woman, the mother of three children, none of whom were in our program, read about the plan in the *Toledo Blade* and wrote us a letter: "Thank you, Thank you, Thank you! . . . I'm impressed and moved to tears of joy by your generosity. I realize the importance of a good solid education, as well as the motivation efforts needed to encourage success. This letter isn't designed to solicit, but to express sincere heartfelt thanks."

From the beginning, we were heavily involved with the students and their lives at school and at home. I hired a full-time coordinator to look after them in school, to follow them, guide them, and make sure they did their homework. We helped them in all sorts of ways, from buying milk and bread to paying rent for parents who could not meet their bills. We were very focused on providing academic, social, and economic help.

The parents could either pay a nominal fee for their children to attend a Catholic school or work part time at the school for payment of tuition. Their work often included cleaning or maintenance.

But while the parents were initially excited, it became difficult as we went along. Some moved away, others would not help out at school. Others got mad at the school and took their children out for silly reasons, mainly the discipline imposed by the nuns.

Dee became a great supporter despite her original misgivings. She would send birthday cards to the children. We would take the kids to the lake and to cultural events. We talked to them continuously and tried to help them work through the problems they faced.

In one case, we had a young man who was president of the freshman and sophomore class at Central Catholic High School. Jermain had good grades and was a football player. During his sophomore year, he began missing out on many school activities and was not fulfilling his leadership responsibilities so was asked to step down. I went to his house and found him taking care of his younger brother and sister because his mother had recently gotten divorced, was working the second shift at her job and needed Jermain to babysit. His job now, as he saw it, was to look after his siblings.

I knew I couldn't just let Jermain drop out of the program. So I waited for his mother to come home, and when she arrived, I told her she had to find someone, whom I would pay, to take care of the other children, because her son would be returning to school the next day. As a single mother, she had not realized the responsibility for his siblings was affecting his school activities. She was able to switch to an earlier shift. That enabled Jermain to stay after school, practice football and once again be part of school activities.

Jermain eventually graduated and was awarded a scholarship to Ohio State University. When he graduated from college, he went to work for Fifth Third Bank. My advice to this young man: Pursue an independent business career.

Another success story was a young man named Juan. His parents had entered the United States illegally to find work picking crops. They eventually established a business supplying groceries to other migrant workers, then turned that into a small market in one of the worst parts of Toledo. Their son who joined our program was one of 11 children in the family. He graduated from college with a degree in criminal justice. As Juan neared graduation, I took him to meet the sheriff of Lucas County, which surrounds Toledo.

Juan asked, "Can I get a job with your department?"

The sheriff said, "Let's see, you have a 3.2 grade point average in criminal justice, and you're Hispanic. You could start tomorrow."

Juan and his family were thrilled.

We had lots of other fine young people in the program, but we also struggled with a number of others who were trying to find their way. Many had a tough time with their classes. The grade school was a good environment because it was a traditional Catholic institution, with nuns who helped the children and pushed them to do well in school. With Sister Audrey, for instance, they all learned algebra, even though it was a foreign language to many of the students. But the high school was less successful. The group became dispersed, and I blame myself for not doing more to ensure they had a better high school experience.

The plan for them after graduating high school was to go to the University of Toledo, which is an open enrollment university. That meant all they had to do to get into the college was graduate from high school. Some students received scholarships and elected to go elsewhere. Out of the original 30 students, 22 graduated high school and went on to college. Sixteen of the 22 students received a college degree. I'm still in contact with a number of them.

Jim Seneff, head of the CNL Real Estate Group in Orlando, summed it up for me. He asked if I had spent a million dollars on the project.

I said, "Probably."

His response: "How better could you spend a million dollars than changing the lives of a group of young people?"

One interesting thing to me during this process was that many of the parents stopped supporting their children when they got out of high school. Perhaps I should not have been surprised, since my parents did the same. Perhaps the students' parents felt they had contributed enough and that it was time to use their money for their own purposes. Certainly that was the case with my father.

Even without financial support, expectations can make all the difference. My mother and father had graduated from university, and although I grew up without much money, there was no question in my parents' minds that I was somehow going to go to college. That kind of support, expectation, and family history can make a huge difference. **If the vision is there, you can follow the path to education and success.**

Even though we were paying for their college tuition, the kids did not have any resources to get there or to buy food or clothes. I think many of the parents—most of whom had not gone to college—did not really expect these kids to continue their education.

One of the students, a basketball player, got a scholarship to study engineering at Ohio Northern University. He flunked out. Then he came back to our coordinator and said he wanted to go to the University of Toledo. When I called his previous college to obtain his transcript for the transfer, they said they needed about $2,000.

I called the student's father, who was employed, and explained to him that if he wanted his son to finish school, he needed to provide the $2,000 to get the transcript. The father said he could not do that, so I made a deal with him. I would pay the money, but if the student went back to college and was not successful, the father would have to repay me.

Ultimately, the student failed again. He could not come to grips with the needs of college study. I did not try to collect, because, even though it was very much like a business contract, the process of putting these students through school felt like a duty to me. I just wanted to help them.

Sponsoring a class from grade school through college proved to be more difficult than I thought it would be. There was much more to it than I originally expected.

I had heard the stories of others who had done this sort of thing, and I had realized I could not just stand up in front of a class of kids and tell them they were going to college. But I did not realize the full expense associated with it, or that the parents, through indifference and neglect, would make it so difficult for their children to receive a free education. Partially, it was because the parents and the kids were not accustomed to the idea of college. It was a foreign concept to them, and because of that, the parents sometimes made it difficult for the children to succeed.

We had a student who wanted to finish college and go to law school, but he was struggling to get his coursework done. His parents were charging him for room and board, so to help him pay his bills, I got him a job at our law firm. As he was trying to work, pay his parents, and get through school, it is not hard to see how difficult it was for him.

I spoke to the parents and tried to help them understand how they were making it hard for their son to finish college and qualify for law school—but they did not seem to care. He did not finish at the university and never became a lawyer.

In some cases, the grandparents were more interested than the parents. Actually, some of these young people lived with their grandparents. Most, however, were from single-parent households, and their mothers, as a rule, cared, but were distracted by trying to get through life. These things can derail a child's track to success. It is so easy to get off-track and just abort your education.

We had young women in college who really wanted to graduate, but they were on the wrong path. One got pregnant, so we supported her through college. But it was very difficult for her. We had another student, a young man who was about to graduate from a two-year program, who suddenly quit to get married to a girl he met working at Burger King, and then worked to support his new family.

The whole process was very much akin to starting a new business—and I learned some vital lessons.

For example, I thought the board we established initially—people of my age or thereabouts—would be effective in mentoring these kids. Yet the mentors who were most effective were the students from the University of Toledo. They were closer in age to the kids. If I could start over, I would pick students younger than the third or fourth grade, probably in kindergarten. An earlier start is essential in making sure they have the necessary reading and math skills. Trying to teach them to read in the fourth grade is exceptionally hard.

My friend Jeb Bush established a law in Florida as governor that if you could not read at the end of the third grade you were held back. This seems hard-line, but it has been effective and has not permanently stigmatized those who had to repeat the grade. Children can learn so much more easily if they're taught to read when they are younger.

Also, I would have opted to put the children in a smaller, private high school. They would have gotten further along than they did in a big school. They were in fairly good shape when they finished the eighth grade, but they did not progress in high school the way they should have. The teachers did not single them out for being in our program. To them, they were just average students in a big city school.

I also could have done more with the mentors and with the supervisor/coordinator during the high school years. I should have been aware of all the potential personal setbacks that posed threats to the success of these students. One of the reasons our schools are as bad as they are is because children, parents, and teachers have so many things to deal with outside of academics.

In the end, though, I found it to be an effective way of getting children into college. It works, but only if you cross all the t's and dot all the i's, and navigate through all the forces working against you: the parents, economic situations, the transitional nature of families over a long period of time, and the family dynamics. I found I was often acting as a facilitator and a marriage counselor. You cannot just say, "I'll provide money for the children to go to college." You have to be involved in many ways throughout the entire process, from grade school through college. Some who did not finish were surely improved by the challenge, anyway.

Still, for me, it was definitely worth it to help these students. It helped change their lives and the lives of others. It will affect the lives of their children and their children's children. I do not think I'll ever know what the full ripple effect will be.

It was difficult for my wife to justify the expense and efforts. She felt that, in the long run, it was not as effective as it should have been. Her thought was that with all that time, effort, and money, we should have gotten more kids through college. But even if it was not the number I had hoped for initially, I do not think it was a foolish endeavor. It was the right thing to do, and I think we helped many kids in the process. I even helped mentor a couple of other people who were interested in taking on the same kind of project after we did.

In hindsight, I recognize I probably should have consulted an organization with similar goals before trying to reinvent the wheel.

This was not entrepreneurship in the classic sense. But the experience drew on everything I had learned as an entrepreneur. If you see a problem, you gather resources to solve it.

I succeeded in some areas and failed in others but made sure to look dispassionately at what I achieved and to share everything I learned. I stepped beyond my comfort zone and immersed myself in a new set of challenges at an age when many of my peers were thinking of retirement. And that was just the beginning of a new life.

My partner and I started eight charter schools in Toledo, and I began one at Sterling College. Letting people manage without constraints in education is a good idea. Exciting venues exist in education today. I heard the president of a local liberal arts college, a very successful school, say their business plan doesn't work. It costs too much to come to the school, students must borrow too much money, and the time duration is excessive.

One innovative solution to that problem is putting educational content online without cost to the person enrolled, in a massive open online course (MOOC). Harvard and MIT are among the schools currently doing so, and they are now finding ways to test the individuals who take those courses and give them credit. Using that as a basic concept, the education system can change. If you can take the courses without charge and get the credit without going on campus, you are in a different world. It is also demonstrable that online education is the equivalent to that in brick-and-mortar colleges.

The present Florida governor, a Republican, had a key guy call me to say he was looking for support from Democrats as he prepared for reelection. He asked if I wanted to be appointed to any one of various boards in the Orlando area and I said "no" since the only thing that really interested me was the Florida Virtual School. Essentially, Governor Jeb Bush and his team had found a successful way to educate K-12 students online. The instructors communicate effectively with the individuals, give them the right content, and allow them to learn at their own pace—and at the time of day that suits them.

After being immersed in the educational system on several levels for many years, and, at age 61, looking for a new challenge, I decided to go back to school myself.

Education, based on liberal ideas, is a lifelong effort. Learning leads to expanded interest and thus to the acquisition of more knowledge.

ALWAYS REMEMBER:

- Particularly in education, do for others and you will be blessed beyond your dreams.

SEVEN

BE A LIFELONG LEARNER

"Conformity is the jailer of freedom, and the enemy of growth."
—A. A. Milne

"Youth is a quality not a matter of circumstances."
—Frank Lloyd Wright

In 1994—almost four decades after receiving a bachelor's degree from the University of Michigan—I decided to go back to college. I was considering a career in politics and thought a master's in public administration would serve me well.

I set my sights on Harvard University's John F. Kennedy School of Government, and I knew I needed to score high on the GRE standardized admissions test if I were to stand a chance of getting in. With little computer experience, I took the test in a children's learning center in Dayton, Ohio.

After I finished, a message on the screen said, "How'd you do? Do you want us to grade this, or do you want to forget it?"

And I answered, "Grade it."

As I was sitting there, thinking about how I had not given myself much time between taking the test and starting the semester, they graded my exam and gave me my scores.

"What schools do you want to send them to?" came up on the screen.

I named only one: Harvard.

My scores were good. Harvard accepted me.

It was already spring, and I told them I'd like to enroll that fall. They told me since it had been such a long time since I had been in school, I would have to attend a summer session to acclimate.

"Either you want me or you don't want me," I told the registrar. "And if you want me, I'm going to come the day before classes start. You decide and let me know."

I showed up the day before classes started in 1994, and they let me in.

At the age of 29, Dwight Eisenhower's career had stalled. He was frustrated about his career prospects and struggling to advance. At a dinner with General George S. Patton, he met another general, Fox Conner, who would change his life. Conner told Eisenhower to study military history. While many of his fellow officers spent the years between the two world wars carousing in bars, Eisenhower, alongside Patton and Omar Bradley, became, under Conner's direction, keen students of soldiering, technology, and international events. They studied how tank divisions could be used, how to finagle increased budgets out of Congress, and how to manage politicians, all of which would serve them in great stead during the war that would make their names.

I hoped college would be similarly invigorating for me and would send me in a fresh direction, feeling intellectually prepared.

An interesting thing about going to college is that it is not age related. I was treated like a regular college student, and I did what students do: drank beer, ate pizza, and stayed up late to solve the world's problems. In addition to my classes in the Kennedy School, I took classes in some of the other schools at Harvard, including law, architecture, education, and art. I loved the freedom, which was ideal for an entrepreneur. I did a lot of public speaking and acted in plays. I learned to row on the Charles River. All in all, it was a marvelous experience. Harvard may be an ivory tower place, but that is what is great about it. I got to think about things I would never otherwise have thought about. It refreshed my mind.

While at Harvard, a biology professor I met at the home of John Silber, president of Boston University and my mentor, invited Dee and me to dinner. Over drinks, I asked, "Is this a myth? Is Harvard a good school or not?"

He replied that when they had an opening in his department the search committee delivered three people to President Conant. Conant wanted someone else, from Princeton, whom he had picked. Over time, all four candidates were hired, and each became a Nobel Laureate.

He said, "Is Harvard a great school or not?"

The Kennedy School was at the intersection of theoretical and practical politics. Everyone you can think of came there and talked and hung out with us. There was a former US ambassador to China, serving as one of the school's politicians-in-residence, who shared his experiences in Asia. Robert McNamara, the former defense secretary, dropped by and talked candidly about his failures during the Vietnam War. I would go down to Boston's saloons and listen in on the vibrant discussions of local politics. One of the folk heroes at that time was Whitey Bulger. His brother was a prominent elected official who became the president of the University of Massachusetts. Whitney went on the run but was eventually found, captured, tried, and convicted for murder, racketeering, extorion and conspiracy.

My only frustration was dealing with the college bureaucracy, which reminded me of my days in the Navy. Once, when I was taking a course in the education school, I was notified part way through the semester that I was not registered in the class.

I went to the registrar and was told: "You thought that the class was cross-registered, but it's not. You need to talk to the people in the education school and get them to sign this form."

So I went over there and talked to a lady at the desk.

She said, "No, that's not the way it works. You have to take our form, fill it out, and have the Kennedy School of Government approve, then we'll act on that. We'll let you know if we'll let you take the course."

"I'm taking the course," I said.

"Well, that's the way it works over here."

"No. Let me talk to the guy who runs this place."

The woman directed me to a guy in the back, and I explained my situation and said, "I want you to sign this form."

"No, you've got to take my form and fill it out. Take it back to the Kennedy School."

By this time, I was adamant. "No, man, sign the form. I want you to sign it right now." I was bigger than he was, and insistent.

So he signed it, stuttering, "B-b-but I need a c-c-copy."

"Okay, what color is your copy?"

"G-g-green."

I ripped off the green copy, gave it to him and went on my way.

Entrepreneurs have no time for that kind of bureaucratic illogic. They see a desired end result and the path to it and have little tolerance for obstructions and byways.

I finished at Harvard early and sent my last exam in from London, where my daughter and her husband were stationed with British Petroleum. When I went home, I called the registrar's office and asked if I had graduated. A woman in the office said no, that I had failed to pay my term bill, which was $1.26. I told them that on the way out of the door to go to Great Britain, the dean had asked me for five thousand dollars to help a group of Mexican students with their bills since the peso had dropped in value.

"Okay, I owe you one dollar and twenty-six cents, and I just gave five thousand dollars to Harvard University. Can we cancel the amounts out?"

She said she believed I was a generous person, but unless I sent one dollar and twenty-six cents, I would not graduate. I sent her a check. I will speak at Harvard one day and start my talk with this story.

There is always a lot of satisfaction to be had in pursuing an interest, starting out in ignorance and getting to the point of under-standing. My experience at Harvard lifted me out of the business world and gave me the confidence to pursue the new adventure I was planning:

I would use all I had learned and deploy it in the race to become the governor of Ohio.

The direct route to a goal is central to entrepreneurship, disregarding bureaucratic illogic and nonsense. The entrepreneur is always on the edge and makes himself uncomfortable.
That state is important.

ALWAYS REMEMBER:

- If you become a student after a hiatus, which is important in your life, you will find you will be treated as you were in college originally.

EIGHT

FAIL WITH THE BEST INTENTIONS

- Engage in politics and civic life.
- Unite people in a common cause.
- Be fearless about asking for support.
- Never relax when the camera is on you.

After Harvard, I returned home to Ohio in 1995 and began plotting my political course as if it were another entrepreneurial endeavor.

There are those who believe politics and business are best kept apart and others who wish they were more alike. How often do you hear exasperated voters say they wish government were run more like business, with more accountability and transparency and less partisanship? Having been in business for many years, it would be hard for me to boast that the ethics or practices of the business world are superior to those in politics. Instead, my view has always been that the two worlds are intertwined. It is important for business owners, just as it is for any citizen, to be engaged in the political process and, in certain cases, to run for office. If a businessman does not want to engage in politics, decisions will be made that he probably will not like by people he does not respect, and his complaints will go unheard.

In 1959, President Eisenhower sent a fascinating letter to a World War II veteran, Robert Biggs, who had written to him complaining that government had become so complex and impersonal that it no longer seemed connected to the citizens whose interests it was supposed to represent. President Eisenhower conceded that the organization of government and the issues it dealt with had become enormously complex and confusing, but that, he said, was the price of democracy.

He referred Biggs to a book, *The True Believer,* by Eric Hoffer.

"In it," wrote Eisenhower, "he points out that dictatorial regimes make one contribution to their people, which leads them to tend to support such systems—freedom from the necessity of informing themselves and making up their own minds concerning these tremendous complex and difficult questions. But while this responsibility is a taxing one to a free people, it is their great strength as well—from millions of individual free minds come new ideas, new adjustments to emerging problems, and tremendous vigor, vitality and progress."

There are clear differences between business and politics and obvious reasons why entrepreneurs find politics so hard. The most obvious difference is in control.

Politics, as Eisenhower wrote, is much less susceptible to control than either business or the military, where he had made his name. An entrepreneur gets used to controlling his environment. In politics, he must make compromises to achieve what he wants. A story about Franklin Roosevelt illustrates how the most successful politicians are often those with the fewest ideological axes to grind.

Roosevelt read hardly any philosophy or poetry, preferring history. He chafed at intellectual discussion. Once, an aggressive young reporter asked him, "Mr. President, are you a Communist?"

"No."

"Are you a capitalist?"

"No."

"Are you a socialist?"

"No," said FDR.

"Well, what is your philosophy then?"

"Philosophy?" asked the president, puzzled. "Philosophy? I am a Christian and a Democrat—that's all."

My only political office to that point had been as a precinct committeeman. I was a Democrat in a Republican village, Ottawa Hills. When I went to my first central committee meeting and arrived late, they told me they had just taken a vote on an issue and of the 30 people there, 15 had voted for and against.

They passed out the ballots again, and I turned mine in blank.

The chairman of the party came up to me and said, "Douglas, did you lose your pencil?"

I told him I didn't understand the issue.

He explained it to me and told me how he thought I should vote. I voted that way the next round and the issue passed 16-15.

A couple of weeks later he called me and asked if I had someone I wanted appointed to the county engineer's office. I didn't, but I learned something in that process.

I embarked on my political career late in life, knowing what the challenges would be. I figured that of all the jobs in politics, the governorship was best suited to my talents, as it was the only state office where you had some measure of control.

Organizing and running a political campaign required many of the entrepreneurial skills I had developed in business. You start with a concept, an idea that you believe in, along with the confidence that you can make a difference. Then you have to share the vision of who you are and what you can do in order to get people's support.

This is marketing and selling.

When my campaign team wanted to focus my attention on the brutal deadlines that are elections, they would say: "We're holding a one-day sale on you on election day." The trick would be to get as many people as possible buying what I had to sell on that one day. Fifty percent plus one.

In preparation for my run, I had set up a think tank called the New Ohio Institute, a public policy organization designed to tackle the worst urban problems. This required I find the right staff and have them conduct useful research. I managed to sign up a great board, including three university presidents, heads of major corporations, the head of the Cleveland Foundation, and a leading Jewish intellectual in Toledo.

I remember walking into the office of the president of Kent State University, Carol Cartwright, to ask her to be a trustee, and I heard one of my staff wonder out loud if we were shooting too high.

"Gee whiz," I said, "no one's ever said no to us, and we've been recruiting all over the place."

Sure enough, Carol signed on.

Peter Kelly, a good friend who was then head of the Democratic National Committee, suggested I recruit Joe Gorman, CEO of the auto parts maker TRW, for the board of the institute, and wrote a letter of introduction. Gorman's assistant said I could have ten minutes with him. When we met, Gorman recalled that Kelly was a drunken Irishman in law school at Yale and that he hadn't seen him in 30 years. Gorman didn't really seem to care whether he crossed paths with Kelly again.

Great start.

Two hours later I was still there, and I asked Gorman if he was going to join our board.

"I decided in the first 20 minutes I'd do it," he said. "And it's more fun to talk about public policy matters than about catalytic converters and mufflers."

Dr. John Silber, my mentor in academe, ran for governor of Massachusetts in 1990. He was way ahead until the last week, when he called a reporter stupid and described Bill Weld, his opponent, as "just another orange-headed Wasp." Weld came to Harvard for lunch when I was there and when asked a question about the election, he said he hadn't won the election, but rather, Dr. Silber had lost it in the last few days.

Silber's response was interesting: He said he would do it all over again, knowing he would lose. That, to him, was the value of the experience and commitment.

I started my campaign with old line pros: a former Democratic state chairman and his media guy. They were good people, but if I had gone to young people, in both fundraising and program matters, it probably would have come out better.

People care a lot about public issues, I found out, and are willing to contribute time and talent to solving problems.

I hired Andrew Benson, one of the guys I had met at the Kennedy School, to run the Institute. Andy and I had awful fights about the issues we were examining. We would yell at each other and then agree the only way we got through it was because of the time we had spent together in college. We knew each other well enough to get things done.

Our core issue turned out to be education reform and how to fund it through new taxes. We believed that better education lay in smaller classes of fourteen or so. But this would require transforming how teachers were trained and paid. We came up with a program to fix all of this, but the state would not fund it. I believed that a new sales tax was the best way to fund the much-needed changes. My plan had broad, bipartisan support and later was at the heart of my bid to become the Democratic candidate for governor.

I had a good team in Ohio to manage the politics and deal with the media, the right people around me politically to advise me and keep me out of trouble. It was fascinating to me how you could become a serious candidate and a household name in a relatively short period of time if you did what you had to do—and spent a million dollars. Even then, when you felt your ideas were on target to solve problems, they still may not be the most popular.

But, in politics as in business, leadership is about bringing people together in a common cause that leads to success.

As a candidate, I was under a lot of media scrutiny, and early in the campaign, I relaxed at my press conferences and enjoyed the back and forth a little too much. I did not realize how extraordinarily disciplined a campaign had to be.

I remember speaking to a large group of women and acknowledging the effect women have on our lives. As an example, I told them about my father and how as a school department head, he had men and women working for him. He used to say that men were neither especially loyal nor hard working and needed the occasional kick in the rear. Women, on the other hand, could be petty, and in large groups exceptionally petty. But if you honestly recognized women's efforts, they were loyal and would do all the work for you. This had always worked for him. The only poor management strategy, he would say, was to be in any way "limp-wristed."

When I came off the podium, my campaign manager, Jim Ruvolo, the former Ohio Democratic Party chairman, rushed up to me and said: "You really fouled up. You can't say things like 'limp-wristed.'"

"I was just quoting my father," I told him.

"It doesn't make any difference. You can't say things like that."

I definitely had to learn more discipline in speaking.

I also had to learn to function very differently in politics from the way I functioned in the construction industry.

When things were not going right in my construction business, I had often gone into a roomful of bankers and gone crazy. I would pound the table and curse. It worked. In politics, you could not do that, but I had to learn.

I also had to learn to be quicker on my feet in response to questions.

Once, when I was in Dayton being interviewed by a newspaper reporter, the reporter was tossing me softball questions. Then, out of nowhere, he asked how I felt about the death penalty. I had never really thought about it, but I said, "If I was governor, and some guy on death row had found the Lord, had converted, and was going to follow Christ—and if I was convinced—I could not let the guy be executed."

When I came out of that interview, Jim said, "You were wrong. Eighty-six percent of people in Ohio are for the death penalty. Is that clear to you?"

I said, "Let me go home and think about it."

The next morning, I told him, "When I was a naval officer and I had to learn how to shoot, I had to think about it. As Seabees we trained with the Marines and had to convince ourselves that if the circumstances required, we'd kill somebody. So I'm for the death penalty. How about you?"

"No," said Jim, "not me. I was a conscientious objector during the Vietnam War. So, I'm not for the death penalty. But *you* are."

Luckily, my comments about the death penalty did not affect my campaign.

Despite being a committed Republican, Dee had thrown herself into campaigning for her Democratic husband. One afternoon, we were interviewed by the *Toledo Blade*, which had been very unfriendly to my candidacy. At the time of the interview, Dee was running three alternative-to-abortion clinics, which I was funding. These were places where a girl could come in and get a pregnancy test. If she was pregnant, we would encourage her to consider options other than abortion.

In the interview, the interviewer asked us, "How do you feel about abortion?"

I said, "Abortion is the law, and if I was the governor, I wouldn't change it. A priest would say you must change the attitude of the public before you can change the law."

Afterward, Dee said, "I didn't know you felt that way. You're opposed to abortion, aren't you?"

"I am," I told her. "But I wouldn't try to change the law because I don't think it can be done."

Fortunately, we could have those kinds of discussions without either of us raising our voice.

Dee was marvelous in the campaign. She could stand there and shake hands with two hundred people. She could dance with them and was good in all sorts of social settings. I think she liked the thought of me running for governor even though she thought it was feckless, which it was. But she is definitely a woman who can rise to the occasion.

Campaigning was a lot of fun. Everyone wants to see you and meet you, so even if you are not their favorite it is easy to get involved with various groups. Everyone tells you they are going to vote for you, then most do not. People want to shake your hand, talk to you, size you up, figure out what kind of a crazy person is doing this, live vicariously—except the people who are paid to criticize you, like the newspaper reporters. And your opponent, obviously. You do opposition research on the person you are running against and go through the process as the voter for yourself. Reading personal opposition research is a daunting experience.

I am one of those people who breaks the world down into those you would go on a sailboat with for any length of time and those with whom you would not. I would not have gotten on a boat with my primary opponent.

Then, there are those things that are hard to like about politics. The first is that often what gets rewarded is public perception rather than reality. People look at you, considering if they can perceive you in office in political discourse, it's called "heft." Machiavelli said that everyone sees you as you appear to be, and few really know who you are. People look at everything. In a focus group we conducted, one guy said of me, "look at the size of that guy's ears; that guy needs an ear job." That type of comment is not useful. Sitting talking to a biased newspaper editor is equally painful, because all they want to hear is something they can use against you.

Ultimately, though, what counted was that we started way behind the Democratic candidate who was heavily backed by the party, and we were trying to convince people of the need for higher taxes. These were insuperable obstacles for me. When it was clear my opponent was going to win, I met with my advisors and decided to drop out. We reserved space for an upcoming news conference in the capitol building in Columbus, then went to an event in Cleveland.

At this previously planned event, my friend Peter Kelly, who had been a prominent player in national politics for more than 30 years, was with us. I remember walking across the lawn in Shaker Heights to a house where there were a couple hundred people waiting to hear me speak.

Peter said to me, "Okay, Elephant Ears, let's see if you can tap dance without your shoes on." He meant, could I still motivate people even when I knew the campaign was over?

Afterward, Peter came up and hugged me, telling me I had done a terrific job. He also said he never thought I could do it.

I replied, "You never thought I could? You were one who encouraged me to run!"

Peter said, "You're my friend and you're entitled to all the support I can possibly give."

It's not fun to lose, in politics or in business. The difficult part is afterward. I was a little crazy the first 30 or 40 days after I quit that campaign. I was disoriented. I bought a house on Lake Erie on a whim and went there to rethink and reconstruct things.

How could I have done it differently?

In hindsight, you see other choices you might have made and become more critical of yourself than others are. Even people who have given you a lot of money do not criticize you, although, for them, it is money that disappeared down a rabbit hole.

I remember meeting Alex Sink, who lost the governorship in Florida in 2010 by less than 1 percent of the vote, and she told me that months afterwards she was still waking up in the middle of the night thinking: "55,000 votes." Second-guessing is painful.

In business you make a deal, it works or does not work, and you move onto the next one. The next one is always there for you. In politics, the chances are not as frequent.

But then again, **you learn by trying**. They say in Ohio politics that you have got to lose the big one to win the big one. Sadly, I was too old to run a second time. I would have to spend the next four years calling on county chairmen and political operatives in 88 counties to be ready for a second run.

Nonetheless, my brief experience in electoral politics taught me a lot. I had always thought a person could make a difference in politics and government but only with real effort. And I have always liked people who look at something and think: I can change that. Of course, it is no fun to deal with people who are corrupt, with politicians who take your money and take advantage. But in my experience, there are good people in politics with the right intentions. If you can influence them, or be one of them during your life, you should certainly try to have an impact.

I had an opportunity to do just that in a different way.

Later in my life, I made some investments in alternative sources of energy. My friends and I bought 75 percent of an oil and gas consultancy/operating company in Denver run by my son-in-law, Steve Struna. The oil and gas business is fascinating. We invested $25 million and then another $25 million. A venture capital firm put in $50 million and has just invested another $250 million. A lot of oil and gas is available in this country, and Elgin Energy's consultancy knows how to find it and determine what it takes to extract it.

We came to see that changing the rules concerning how we drilled for oil would make a significant impact on all of us. Steve gave me a fascinating book on reservoir engineering. They do amazing things like water flooding in which they put 100 gallons of water down an old well and extract 101 gallons, the difference being the amount of oil that comes up. At $90 per barrel, that makes sense. It is fun to go out on the rigs and see what they do, to look at the formations and the logs and realize how fracking will bring out gas and oil. The fracturing occurs at such a level that there is no danger to the water supply or other environmental activity.

In the end, no matter what industry you are in, or what successes or failures you have, you can never say government does not matter. It matters hugely. Only government can change fuel economy standards or decide that all new cars should be equipped to run on natural gas; a true game changer. Hopefully, the good people in politics will make the right changes for our future--the first time.

Government ultimately has the biggest lever there is for driving important change.

ALWAYS REMEMBER:

- Informing yourself on complex and difficult questions of public life can be taxing but from free minds come new ideas, new adjustments to emerging problems and tremendous vigor.

- If you don't engage in politics and solve problems, someone will dictate solutions that you will have to endure.

- Politics creates scrutiny and personal introspection; it's different from industry and causes you to rethink your beliefs.

NINE

TAKE A CHANCE — THEN KNUCKLE DOWN

"The greatest managers in the world do not have much in common. They are of different sexes, races, and ages. They employ vastly different styles and focus on different goals. But despite their differences, these great managers do share one thing: Before they do anything else, they first break all the rules of conventional wisdom."
—Marcus Buckingham and Curt Coffman
in *First, Break All the Rules*

"Hang a lantern on your problem."
—Robert F. Kennedy

With a PhD, the critical ingredient, I felt I could become a college president. My previous specific experience was as a university trustee for 11 years (and for 6 of those years board chairman) and a short period as the president of the University of Toledo when the incumbent was ill. The opportunity to improve the academic life, finances, faculty, and facilities of a college was important to me.

Before my search for a college presidency started, in 2000, well before my doctorate in 2004, a friend who was on the board of the state university in New York said to me, "Why not apply for the presidency of Bernard Baruch College in Manhattan? It has a public-policy school, business department, and a liberal-arts program. You have all those covered."

I asked my friends in academe if that was a good idea, since I didn't have a PhD. They said, "You have zero chance at that position."

Nonetheless, I applied. Late in 2000, a headhunter from Korn/Ferry called me and asked that I put on one piece of paper why I should be president of the school. After that, in December, she said they had narrowed the list to five finalists and the interviews would start in January. That seemed like a good time to ask my wife if she wanted to live in Manhattan for five years or so.

She replied, "If you go to New York you will go with some other woman."

That didn't seem like a good idea to me so I told the Korn/Ferry woman to cross me off the list.

That decisive step put me on a path that led us to Kansas. I wasn't the Wizard of Oz and Dee wasn't Dorothy, but the transition was equally bizarre.

Seven months earlier, Dee and I had left Ohio for deepest Kansas—four hours' drive from Kansas City, well into Midwestern farm country. I had taken on the job of president of Sterling College, a small Presbyterian liberal arts college just as it faced a slew of problems.

"Boss, we're broke," my chief administrator told me.

Money, as the administrator told me that cold morning in my office, was the first problem—but that was just the start of it. Enrollment was down to 450 students. The admissions office was offering scholarships and tuition discounts they could not afford. The facilities were aging and poorly maintained. The faculty was both mediocre and entitled, a deadly combination. And morale was terrible.

A few years before, my son Peter and I had opened an office in Orlando, Florida, where the weather is better and the commercial opportunities abundant. It would have been tempting at that point in my life to retreat to the balmy warmth of central Florida and kick up my heels. At 72, I had earned it.

But I wanted another big job. I had sought out this challenge, just as I had looked for challenges throughout my life, and now Sterling College's problems were mine to solve.

"Courage in solving problems," Socrates said, "requires the ability to distinguish between real and perceived threats. You must know what should be feared and what should not be. What should not be feared can be forgotten; what is to be feared must be surmounted."

With that in mind, I set about my work.

By this time, 2005, I should note I was no longer just Mr. Bruce Douglas; I was now Dr. Douglas, having acquired a PhD. I had long wanted to be a college president, but knew I lacked the academic credentials. So I set about acquiring my doctorate with the same kind of discipline I had shown building shopping centers. I finished my basic coursework at the graduate school at the University of Toledo, and before writing my dissertation, I asked my mentor Dr. John Silber what it would take to get it done. His advice was concise: I had to have a reason for doing it, and I had to know what I was going to do. I needed to write 20 pages every day, to start at seven o'clock every morning and do nothing but write. I shouldn't wait until I felt the spirit move me or until I felt I completely understood something.

The research was interesting. Nicolas Biddle, my uncle who was the focus of my dissertation, was a legendary banker of the early 19th century. When I went to Philadelphia to study his life and career, I met, for lunch, another descendant named Anthony Drexel Biddle IV. His father had been the ambassador to the governments in exile in World War II. He suggested I go out to the Biddle estate, where his uncle, James Biddle, was still in residence.

When I showed up there, the woman taking care of the place told me my uncle's papers had never been organized or cataloged. She went into the basement, attic, closets, and garage to find his documents. I sat in his office along the Delaware River and did the study. It was my thought that the historiography surrounding Biddle's fight with Andrew Jackson was inadequate. Jackson put Biddle out of business by refusing to recertify the Second Bank of the United States, and it was hard for me to believe that two people so adept in the political arena could get in that sort of a fight.

Following Silber's advice, I sat at my computer each day and wrote 20 pages on Nicholas Biddle, the head of the Second National Bank of the United States. By 10 o'clock each morning, I was pretty well burned out, my mind swimming with information about inflation, money supply, commodity prices, and gold. I would close it out, go back the next morning, edit, and write another 20 pages. Before long it was done.

The outside reader for my dissertation was the head of the economics department at the University of Toledo. I had developed formulae on prices, money supply, and inflation that fit the empirical data. However, he thought he knew more about those topics than I did, and that led to some contentious discussions.

Finally the head of my dissertation committee told him: "This guy walks at commencement on April 17."

I had my doctorate.

My path to Sterling was less direct. In my search for a college presidency, I had hired a consultant who told me what I already knew: **I was a very unconventional candidate.** No college was likely to hire me without strong recommendations from people they knew. Although my experience in college administration was limited, I nonetheless interviewed for posts in New Mexico, New York, Washington, and even Alaska.

Over dinner in Alaska, one of the female trustees of the college considering me asked if I would be willing to become the president of Sheldon Jackson College if they offered me the position.

I replied, "You're a lovely woman. If a man asked if you'd marry him if he asked you, how would you respond?"

The consultant called me the next day and said, "I know you were helping me and didn't want the job. You escaped. But let me tell you. The answer to the question of would you take the job if it was offered to you is yes, even if you don't want it."

As I had learned in politics, construction does not prepare you to say the "right" thing every time.

I was contacted in 2005 by some former classmates from Harvard who asked me to help them with a company they were forming to establish a distance-learning program. They had contacts with military organizations involved in educating students in the Army, Navy, and Air Force on a number of bases.

They wanted to develop their program by affiliating with a college or university for the necessary accreditation to give college degrees online. I was not really interested in running their company, but I wanted to help them, and I thought I could give advice. So, I joined them in a meeting with the trustees of Sterling College, a liberal arts school in Kansas affiliated with the Presbyterian Church. The business part of the meeting came to nothing, but a short time afterward, one of the trustees, Tony Thompson, a real estate entre-preneur from California, called a good friend of mine and said: "We need to have Bruce come to Sterling to be our president."

I said to tell the guy that if he would put a million dollars in the First National Bank in Sterling for me to use to help the college, I would take the job.

I did not expect him to do that, but he did.

The trustees invited me to come back to Sterling for a formal interview. Dee said, "I'm not going to live in Kansas." Yet she agreed to make the trip.

I reminded the trustees of what I said about the million dollars for Sterling—and I told them I only wanted to be considered for the job if they went through a search process and interviewed other candidates.

Dee warmed to the idea. When we were being interviewed by one of the various constituent groups, she whispered to me to ask if they had coed dorms.

They said, "No. We don't believe in that."

Neither did she. She fist-pumped under the table. There are now two dorms at Sterling College named after us, one for men and one for women, which we built in our time there.

On our first trip to Sterling, the people were very nice and encouraging. But on our way home my plane hit bad weather, and we had to fly around a storm and got home late. Dee hated flying anyway, and I thought this was a bad omen. But at seven o'clock the next morning, our daughter from Chicago called at the office and said, "Mummy is ready to go to Kansas."

I said, "Really?"

"Yep," she replied, "but she says you don't want the job."

Actually, I did want the job.

It was offered to me in August 2005, and I agreed to start a month later.

"It is an honor to be chosen to serve as president of Sterling College," I said in a press release. "Liberal arts education informed by Christian beliefs is important. Science determines too many aspects of our life, and scientific discovery requires a search for meaning in order to guarantee its use for good. Reason and revelation go together with a historic Christian commitment to the relationship of faith and reason. I will seek respect and empowerment of others at Sterling through charisma empowered by Christian leadership."

Taking on the challenge at Sterling would give me yet more of what I wanted out of my life. I would be out of my comfort zone. I would have a chance to help people. I would be taking risks and making a difference.

Everything I claimed I stood for, all the skills I thought I had, would be tested yet again.

When I told an old friend of my plans to take the job at Sterling, he told me: "This isn't much crazier than other things you've done."

I think he was saying there are things inside and outside your comfort zone. I had always sought to do things outside my comfort zone, but not so far outside it was ridiculous. I was not trying to be a pop star, or the punt returner for the New York Giants—but I was challenging myself.

To live a fulfilling life, sometimes you just have to grit your teeth and go beyond what you have done previously, as long as it is reasonable and offers a chance of success.

I would not have gone to Sterling to be president without my mentor Jim Fisher having analyzed its strengths and weaknesses and telling me what he thought could be done to make it an effective school. Jim had been president of Towson University and the Council for Advancement and Support of Education (CASE). He has run colleges and written about those experiences and believes firmly that entrepreneurs make the best college presidents.

In support of my presidency, he wrote:

"We found in our study (of college presidents) . . . that the effective college president was entrepreneurial. We also found in two studies that less than 20 percent of the sitting presidents are effective in this country. . . Boards typically appoint the wrong person. . . (Bruce) fits the mold of the entrepreneurial president in the one word—risk. And risk-taking is a very important characteristic. . .

He also inspires his people. They respect him and they like him because they know he cares about them."

Jim believed that the same qualities I had shown as an entrepreneur would help me succeed at Sterling: "First, is courage—and enough to really press on. Next is intelligence, and the next is compassion. Intelligence means you're smart enough to know what you're doing. Compassion is terribly important as you move forward... Then he comes out with those characteristics as a very charismatic figure. He has the ability to inspire trust and confidence. And charisma is amoral. It's not moral or immoral, but all persons who have that quality—that enables them to move people beyond themselves. That's Bruce."

When you need to step outside your comfort zone and take risks, you need help and a way of measuring what you are facing. Again, entrepreneurship is not about taking any old risk but about managing the risks you deem worthy of taking.

But, of course, you can always be surprised.

I knew the situation at Sterling was grim. But just how grim I would quickly find out. Fortunately, I had Jim Fisher to advise me during my first year. He's a Marine, with all of the characteristics of that breed. The routine was for him to call at 7 a.m. on Thursdays. At that time every day, a siren rang out in the town of Sterling. Before it ended, Fisher was always on the phone. Each Tuesday night I prepared for a grilling, and the next day he would tell me where I was off base.

"Go into the president's office and act as if you know how to do the job," he told me when I started work at Sterling. "Nobody will gainsay your reason for being in charge." His advice reminded me of the "honest arrogance" approach I had used when starting out in business for myself.

Every entrepreneur needs the command of an honest arrogance to convince others of their abilities before they've had a chance to prove them.

There are four key ingredients in the success of a college or university; they all start with "F" and they are all words you can tell your mother: faculty, facilities, finances, and freshmen. My first few months were focused on restoring Sterling's financial health.

I called all the Sterling staff and faculty together in the auditorium to tell them about the financial difficulties. We were broke. We did not have credit, even with the local bank. The college had done several projects, including renovation of the grand old building on campus called Cooper Hall, but had run into trouble during the process and borrowed a lot of money. So we had debt that had to be restructured.

Openness in difficult situations is always the best policy. When John Kennedy was struggling to overcome public suspicion of his Catholicism, his brother Bobby advised him to "hang a lantern on your problem," by which he meant do not try to avoid it, but rather bring everyone's attention to it. There was no shame in being a Catholic, so Kennedy should feel free to be open and challenge any prejudice. I chose to hang a lantern on Sterling's financial problems in the hope that it would rally people to help resolve them.

"Bear with me. Together we'll fix this," I said.

Of course, they had heard that from others in the past and were skeptical about the outcome. But the reality was harsh and many people in the college were simply ignoring it, hoping it would go away—a disastrous approach to any problem.

We would have to raise a lot of money, about four to five million dollars a year. Much of that would have to come from people who were not alumni and who were outside the Presbyterian Church. Sterling alumni were not big givers, and the Presbyterian Church contributed little—in fact, the church had reneged on its initial capital promise to the school in 1785.

To raise what we needed, we would have to go where the money was. And that was usually a long way from rural Kansas. My personal diary quickly filled up with stories about the endless travel, the long drives to meet potential donors with no guarantee of success.

WHAT I'VE LEARNED ABOUT RAISING MONEY

Over the years I have raised around $50 million for various causes, ranging from non-profits to my run for governor. I have learned quite a bit during that process.

To solicit funds is not to go, cap in hand, begging support for some marginal activity. It is, instead, to invite a friend to share in the privilege of the greatest partnership of all.

"The quest for knowledge on which our present existence and our future well-being depend," Frank H. T. Rhodes, president emeritus of Cornell University, put it.

I never left a meeting without asking for money and would say, tongue in cheek, "I'm a college president; I *have* to ask for your support."

If you tell people you are broke and need their money, they will ignore you. Everyone has needs and poverty is a downer. But if you tell people your story and involve them, and if they are convinced lives will be improved, they will give you money.

You have to make a direct link between money
and what it can do.

Fundraising is basically sales. People will only donate if they believe their gift will make a difference. You have to show them the change and improvement that will result. I had to create a whole new group of donors by finding out, with the help of the trustees, who had money, and then ask them to help us. Usually they were not alumni and were not affiliated with the college. They were just people like the McVays, local community members that were not alumni, but had the desire and the means to help us make a difference--and believed in us.

At one point, I wanted to replace the head of our business school, who I thought was incompetent. In private conversation about the man, I used to say that he had gotten his PhD in a Cracker Jack box. But I would need to fund a new, endowed chair in order to attract someone with the talent I felt the job deserved. I found my man, a great professor named Kevin Hill. When I interviewed Hill and asked him to come, he said that he wanted to go home and talk to his wife in Southern California. I said he could not do that, that he had to sign right then. Kevin did.

Now I needed the money for the chair. I turned to Peter and Mary McVay, who had lived in the area but were not alumni. Peter had been president of the Cargill Company in Minneapolis, the largest privately held corporation in the United States. At one time, I called Peter at his ranch in Australia, where he spends part of the year.

He said, "Let me get Mary on the phone."

I thought I was in trouble. With both of them listening, I explained I couldn't hire Hill without a donation of $1.5 million.

Peter said, "Let me see, Bruce. I think you want me to give you money, don't you?"

I replied that was exactly what I had in mind.

Peter laughed and agreed.

The McVays came to Sterling, met the Hills, and then, after dinner that evening, Peter put his hand on my shoulder and shook the other hand, saying he was very glad he had come. We would have the money. My two 80-year-old benefactors then walked down the sidewalk hand in hand. It was one of the better days for the school and for me. The McVays had made a difference, and they had seen from Kevin Hill and his wife Stephanie that we had enhanced the standards of the school and the education of our students.

BOILED FROG SYNDROME

Interestingly, a number of students did not agree with replacing the incumbent head of the business program. A group of them came to my office to complain. I asked them to wait and see what a dramatic positive change this would engender in the fall. Students have a familiarity with a certain individual and stick with him. It is the "boiled frog" syndrome: a great time in moderate heat will cause the animal to cook to death in a pan, though a lot of heat in short order will make the frog jump out.

Meeting student groups head-on to hear their objections is important.

The trustees themselves did not contribute or raise much money. Neither did the alumni, who were mostly teachers and preachers. This was a problem because it gave the impression they did not believe in us themselves.

I tapped every source I could. I remember going to a guy in Wichita, Fred VanBebber, who was a University of Kansas graduate. I asked him for $50,000.

At first, he declined, saying, "I'm not going to give you $50,000 today."

I replied that if he did not give it today, I would come back the next day and ask him again. I kept after him, and he finally donated and has continued to support the school.

Before going to Sterling, I had gone to Jim Seneff, the friend in Orlando, and told him I needed a million dollars for scholarships, and that if he would give $100,000 a year for five years, I would match it personally. He did it the first year, but the next year he said he felt he could not contribute because I was a director of his company. He would have to continue his donations when I was no longer president of Sterling. I put in his share during that time, and he is now making it up. It is great to be able to say to Jim that I carried him through this process, though his resources are greater than mine.

I raised a lot of money, and I do not think fundraising is particularly hard work. You just have to be diligent about it. It is an intricate process. But I met all kinds of nice people and received lots of help.

One of the people I met was the editor and publisher of the newspaper in Winfield. Sometimes, fundraising can be expensive. I learned this the hard way after meeting the publisher for lunch in Winfield. As I drove through the next town--Douglas, Kansas--I was stopped for speeding.

"This is confusing: You have Ohio license plates, a Florida driver's license, and you're in Kansas," he told me.

I acknowledged that it was confusing to me as well.

That did not stop him from giving me a ticket for going 83 miles per hour in a 55 mile per hour zone.

Once we were on decent financial footing, I went to the bank and told them we were experiencing financial shortfalls during the summer before tuition was paid in the fall. I needed a line of credit. I was having a hard time understanding why the bank would not give it to us. After all, I had $5 million in lines of credit in my business that I was not using.

The bankers said the circumstances were different. I acknowledged that was true but told them they should sign us up, regardless, and help us. And they did. The bankers finally realized we were on the rise and their money was safe.

In nonprofits as in business,
it helps to have the banks on your side.

With our finances more secure, we could move on to fixing the rest of the college. People said, in an admiring way, that I was running the college as a business. Actually, a business has money as an input and output measure. For a college or university, money is an input measure but the output is what the students have learned—basically, their understanding of the meaning of life and their technical skill. **Strategically, success in academe is fairly simple; it is principally good students interacting with great faculty.**

When in a tight spot that needed to be made light of, I used to declare that I had been backed up against a wall with my belly button in touch with my backside before and had always managed to work my way out.

But fixing Sterling was an entirely new kind of challenge, requiring creativity as well as money. Fortunately, I liked being in that situation. I have always enjoyed solving complex problems. Beyond complexity, there is usually a simple answer. Starting companies is a challenge; motivating inner-city kids is daunting; politics on the state level is difficult; promoting statewide public policy solutions is not easy; and implementing radical structural engineering practices invites critics.

Sterling was no different.

A big part of the challenge was simply adapting to the unique culture of a college campus. If the weather's particularly fine, it has long been a habit of mine to greet people by saying, "Terrible day, isn't it?" Back home, people got my sarcasm. In Sterling, my greeting elicited downcast looks. Finally, I asked a student what the problem was. He told me that because I was an authority figure, if I said it was a bad day, it must be.

Leadership can be lonely work, and I discovered the gravity of this problem at a retreat for Christian college presidents. The men there complained bitterly about the isolation they felt and the difficulty of their work. Either they were considered too Christian or not Christian enough. They were guiding the college in the right or wrong direction. One guy talked about how he had hired a psychiatrist to help him through, while another said he prayed nonstop, saying, "Lord, I cannot do this job."

It was never so bad for me, but I could see where they were coming from. I remember being visited by faculty and students who told me Sterling was not Christian enough, faculty who complained about their salaries, and department heads with personal financial problems, all with their own view of what Sterling should be doing.

I wrote in my journal: "It's like the manufacturing firm in which the engineers just want to sell to the people who appreciate the wonderful features of the product (faculty); the accountants only want to sell to people who pay their bills (CFO); the manufacturing types only want the people who recognize quality to buy (administrators); and the sales folks want to sell to everybody (admissions)."

I sometimes wished I could have talked to my father. He knew about education and the problems I was facing, and he might have been able to help me. Finally, we could have something we could talk about without all the baggage that burdened our relationship. Unfortunately, he was gone by then. Pop had insight into the faculty problems, with both men and women in his department, which could have helped me. Timing is everything, though, and if he had been willing to impart his knowledge, I was probably not in a position to receive it, psychologically.

It was up to me to see the whole picture and press forward on Sterling's behalf.

As enrollment grew, at one point we needed more dormitories but had no credit to build them. The trustees said we did not need new dormitories, since we were not filling the ones we had, but I knew we were going to grow and would require them.

So I went to a developer and said, "If you'll build us a couple of dormitories, we'll put students in those rooms first before we fill ours up. But I can't sign a lease and I can't do any financing."

Surprisingly, the developer did it, and it worked out. It was a unique arrangement: no financial commitment other than that our students occupy the rooms. The developer did the financing, we ran the dormitories, and it all worked. When we left, they named the dormitories after Dee and me. They are *not* coed.

When the dormitories were finished, one of the students, the captain of the soccer team, called me and said he had bugs, probably because we had not planted the lawn as yet. I suggested that he and his pals come to our house and stay, but he declined. A little later he asked me to come and stay with them for the night. I asked the theater department to give me an outfit that would make me look like a bug, went to the pizza joint downtown for ten pizzas, and walked across campus to their room. Students who saw me must have thought I was crazy, but I stayed up late with the soccer captain and his dorm mates talking about the problems of the world.

At the end of the discussion, he said, "That's your bunk over there, let's turn in."

With communication and without pretense, people will learn your true self. As for the soccer team captain's problems with bugs, once the sod was installed, the problem went away.

I tried to be equally open in every area of my work. People frequently wandered into my office and that was okay. I needed to talk to them. I could not be isolated in my position. If a student wanted to talk, I would talk. If a student had a complaint, I would answer the complaint.

Once I had an issue with the head of the student government. I thought the woman was doing a lousy job. So I brought her in, and we talked about it. I criticized her.

She did not like me doing that, and she showed her dissatisfaction for months—but she changed. She decided to run for the position again the next year, after asking for permission, and she was elected. She performed much better.

HE WAS RIGHT AND I WAS WRONG

Students, I discovered, react strongly and emotionally to campus events. When I had been on the college grounds for about two weeks, the dean of students told me that a student had put derogatory comments on his Facebook page about another student, and the latter beat him up.

I said we had to throw the second kid out of school because nobody beats up anybody on our campus. The dean anticipated an uproar and a line of complainers. My response? Each complainer could come right in, and I would deal with them when they showed up.

Fortunately, the dean was able to reconcile matters between the two students, who shook hands and exchanged apologies. The dean was right and I was wrong, but I still believe that you must always deal with problems quickly and decisively.

College towns are small places, where it is impossible to hide. People expect a lot of the president. It is not enough for you just to do your job and go home. You are also expected to act as a kind of mayor or ambassador in all that the town does.

When I started, someone told me I had to go to all of Sterling's high school football games and show up at PTA meetings, plays, and the like. Instead, I hired a local man, Paul Bingle, who had been superintendent of the schools, as chief operating officer and asked him to tell me what I had to attend and when I did not have to go. I was not going to spend time in areas where I did not absolutely have to in order to stay in contact with people. So he told me the people with whom I needed to maintain contact and friendships.

But it did not always go smoothly.

One of the more difficult decisions I had to make was in regard to the athletic director of the college. He was a long-time favorite of the people in the town and on campus, but he was not doing his job properly. He did not adequately control the recruiting, the scholarships, or his budget.

I knew my decision to replace him would upset many people, and sure enough, several of them went to one of our trustees and expressed their opposition. The trustee assured them it was something I had to do and told them they should not come and talk to me about it, for their own sake.

The football coach was able to control scholarships and expenses, and I asked him to be the athletic director. All he wanted, really, was to be a Division I football coach. He had me promise the school would be financially stable in a year.

I did.

He said, "I'll do the job. What do you want me to do?"

"All I really want you to do is win football games," I answered.

He said he would do that and all the other stuff too, which he did very well.

It was the same with our football field and track. It was in rough shape and was used by the local high school just as much as we used it. The high school, though, only paid about $3,000 a year towards its upkeep. So when I had to spend $1.2 million to fix it, I went to the high school and asked them to pay half.

Their response: "We shouldn't have to pay that. We don't have the money to do that."

"Well, you'd better find it," I said.

"We have a contract that says we can use it for $3,000 a year for another three years."

I was clear. "Next fall, you're going to play football somewhere else unless you come up with the money."

That agitated the school board and the college trustees as well, who told me I should be more lenient and helpful to the school system. Still, they supported me—and the high school came up with the money.

Small towns come with a lot of entrenched relationships that make it difficult to make changes without ruffling feathers. Kansans, generally, make a quick decision on a person, deciding whether they are worthy of support and friendship, and never change their minds. **But change is hard anywhere without ruffling feathers. Entrepreneurs often live at right angles to the rest of the world. So they need to get used to the feeling.**

I wrote for the local newspaper, *The Sterling Bulletin,* on a regular basis, visited the paper each week when the publisher put it to bed, and kept in regular contact with state legislators. They could not give us much state money, but they gave us a lot of support, and they applauded what we were doing.

I also became close to our congressional representatives. The governor, Kathleen Sebelius, called me at the suggestion of her father, John Gilligan, a friend who had been governor of Ohio when I was there. She eventually established a state office at the college, at my request, and was very supportive. She was an exceptional state leader, a Democrat in a red state. Kansas politics were friendly and open then, which was a pleasure. Kathleen tells me that politics in Kansas are now contentious, with groups on the right and left who cannot compromise. She, of course, was head of HHS and faced a similar situation in Washington, DC.

I did what I had to do, and I gained a lot of support. I remember being in the First Presbyterian Church of Hutchinson, Kansas, with a woman who had at first refused to support the college after a poor experience as a trustee and who was now helping us. Before we sat for the service, she told me I was doing a wonderful job and had saved the school.

That sort of conversation goes nowhere, but as the service went along and I prayed, I said to myself, "You know, a number of wonderful things have happened here that I don't understand and can't control, and it must be from the provenance of God." We were blessed.

I spoke at Protestant churches all over the state to gain support. Once, I was to give the sermon at a Presbyterian church in Zenith, a town that was basically a grain elevator and the church. As I approached Zenith, I was e-mailing the athletic director on my Blackberry and missed the entire town. When I got back, I asked the man who was standing outside where the pastor was.

"There is no pastor; you're the one who's conducting the service."

I gave the opening prayers, lead the hymns, gave the children's sermon, the basic sermon, and the benediction. Everyone seemed happy, though I was Catholic and they were not. They took me to lunch and were friendly in the Kansas manner.

Another time I was to speak at the Presbyterian church in a nearby town. My grandson, however, wanted to go to the opening of the World Series in Detroit that day. When my assistant called to postpone, the church official was upset. I called back and said I would come worship with them when we returned, and did so. It seemed more important to go to the World Series with my grandson than to speak at their church, but I never voiced that feeling.

HOW TO FIND GOOD STUDENTS

Increasing enrollment seemed an obvious priority for a college needing to grow. After analyzing all the various costs involved and the ways we could attract more students, I concluded one way would be for the faculty to recruit students they wanted, much in the way athletic coaches do.

The faculty objected. Their job, they said, was to teach. Mine was to deliver the students.

I insisted that was not the way it should work. They had to interact with students, establish confidence, call them, and encourage them to enroll. I told them I would keep track of their efforts and set a quota for each of them.

While some of the faculty did very well, others did not. For the ones who were not so successful, we had an admissions staff member monitor the professor's progress. I was informed of the outcomes, and then it was my job to meet with them, if necessary, and insist they meet quota.

I strongly believed that if a possible matriculant came on campus and met a faculty member, they should work to develop a rapport—because that leads to good students enrolling at the college. Despite the faculty's opposition, the process worked, and our enrollment more than doubled while I was there.

Running a college, I found, had new challenges I never had to worry about in business. As a classic entrepreneur, you make the product, sell it, make money, and make your people happy.

At the college, somebody would give $2,000 to the school and then just show up at my office, unannounced, and want to know how we spent it. They were often quite demanding. **I had more bosses as a college president than I had ever had as a businessman.**

One of my greatest concerns on becoming a college president was working for a board of trustees. An entrepreneur like me is not used to reporting to others before acting. Then there was the faculty, which had three committees: planning, advanced planning, and personnel. We would go to one of the committees, make a deal, and they would then take it to the four divisions, masticate the ideas and submit them to the faculty acting as a committee of the whole. It all took forever.

So I said to the faculty, "We're going to change this to a nine-person faculty senate. We'll have committees, staff them, and will get things done."

They voted unanimously, on paper, not to do that.

I went back to them and said, "The AAUP (American Association of University Professors) rules say I have to take this to the trustees and they will do one of two things, neither of which you will like. Either they will tell me to do it—which is most probable—and I will go ahead and make the changes. They will ask what is wrong with the faculty, anyway? They will trash you. You think they do not respect you, but I am your greatest advocate with them. You do not want to spoil that. Or they will say, leave it the way it is, do not make the changes, and in that case I will quit.

"You don't want either one of those things to happen."

The trustees decided to force the changes, and we had a clean governance system. But the result was acrimony for a year afterward.

It was not always so harmonious between me and the Sterling trustees, either. Six to eight months into my term, the chairman came up with an evaluation system for my performance and said he wanted to post it on the wall during the trustees' meeting. His goal was to have people comment on the scope of my activities and various parts of my job performance, and review the numbers.

I was uncomfortable with the idea of being evaluated in public, and threatened to quit. When they realized we were going in the right direction without the evaluation system, they backed off and let me make the decisions I needed to make. **Thus I was given the entrepreneurial control that was necessary for me to lead and manage.**

I had never worked as president of an organization with a board that operated in the public eye like this college. The trustees felt responsible to a lot of people. I stayed on the right side of the finances and on the right side of the media and worked hard at both. But I still had a lot to learn. My mouth would run away from me occasionally, as it had in politics.

I remember speaking to members of the Rotary Club in Hutchinson, Kansas, and telling them I was going to have to replace a number of "crummy" faculty members. The next thing I knew, my comments showed up on the front page of the Hutchinson newspaper, to my annoyance and that of the trustees.

When I first realized I wanted to be an entrepreneur, it was because I wanted control over my own life. I did not want to spend my time on earth suffering under bad bosses, doing work I did not care for. I wanted to forge my own destiny, to make my own money, solve difficult problems, and, as my father had emphasized, help others in the process.

PUBLIC VS. PRIVATE ORGANIZATIONS

Working with the trustees of a public organization was quite different from working with my board at the Douglas Company. The company board was a high-powered group of people who were strong in their views and critical when I did something wrong. If I had a problem, the Douglas Company board of directors had a program to check periodically to see how I was progressing. I reported to them semi-annually in one form or another—but they did not push, because I owned the company. They advised and consulted.

I do not think most entrepreneurs have directors who tell them very much. They know it is your company and that ultimately you can do what you want. But you want people around you to give you feedback and tell you what you did wrong. You just do not want them to micromanage.

During my time in the Navy, I learned that it was not just about me. Leadership and the management of others is crucial to getting anything done.

My time at Sterling was the summation of that view. I liked that we were helping students, and I enjoyed the challenges. I liked being able to walk into faculty members' offices, talk about their concerns, and have an intellectual discussion. That was a lot of fun. But I was not like most other college presidents, who are usually looking for more praise and more money—and are almost always looking for a bigger job. I did not care about the praise nor did I need money. And I was not looking for another job. I was lucky. I could enjoy the moment.

Peter Drucker said that doing the right thing is more important than doing the thing right. Effectiveness trumps efficiency.

After the faculty senate reorganization, a psychology professor became the recording secretary. In that job, an individual has the right to record what, in his subjective view, happened in a meeting. This man was what we call in the Navy a "sea lawyer," which meant he knew the regulations and could always tell you why you could not do what you planned.

I told the academic dean I would not sign that psych professor's contract for the next year and wanted to get rid of him. The dean said I had to sign it because he had a three-year commitment ahead of him, which was Sterling's answer to tenure.

My answer: "There is no way my arm will pick up a pen and sign that man's contract. It's not physically possible."

The dean asked if he could send the professor in to talk to me.

I said that was wrong for two reasons. First, it would undermine his authority, and second, I might throw him out into the street, and that would cause a controversy.

The dean said that we would probably be sued.

"I've been sued before," I responded, "but never effectively by anyone, and I'm not afraid of being sued again."

The professor did come in, and I told him he was a problem I could no longer tolerate. He asked if I thought he was a good teacher.

I did.

He asked if I believed he was a good recruiter, which was required of all professors.

I did.

He then suggested that if I would sign his contract, he would opt out of the faculty senate and stop being a pain.

I did, and he conformed as he promised. When my wife and I returned to the campus two years later, invited to a football game, he gave me a hug and showed his respect. We did the right thing and it worked out.

I went into the president's job with a three-year plan but never told anybody that. I did not have a contract, and I was not paid. At one point, someone in a trustees' meeting said to me, "The way things are going, we want to get you a contract."

But I did not like the fact that the trustees were giving very little money to the college, and I told them unless they started giving more, I did not ever want a contract. I never thought I needed it. I could afford to do the job without their money. The risk was I could be fired at any time, completely at their discretion. Nobody ever took that step.

As a leader—whether a college president or an entrepreneur—if people like you and want you to be successful, they will follow you. You will be able to make progress and get things done.

It has everything to do with how you relate to people. You need to energize them in a relatively short period of time when you go into a new situation. You have to interact on a daily basis. People quickly know whether you are the genuine article, whether your hands are clean, your heart is pure, and you are trying to do what's best for the organization.

A person's early decision to trust you and follow you usually does not change unless you do something egregious.

I did not have the traditional background of a college president, but in leadership, there was very little adjustment from business to college. It really was not much different—and I used some of the same principles and tactics I used in business and some from the Navy as well.

For example, I would take my staff away before the year started, and we would discuss ideas. We would decide what we were going to do, unify as a group around a plan, and do it.

You want strong people with big egos because these are the people who really care. We had some serious discussions and disagreements, but you want disagreements. You do not want to go into a room and have everybody immediately agree on proposed ideas. You need the discussion and exposure to various viewpoints to establish the best plan and avoid pitfalls. We had the power, as most entrepreneurs do, to meet at seven o'clock on a Monday morning, decide to do something, and implement it an hour later.

The key at the college was for me to find the right people as vice presidents and have everybody agree on the mission and vision of the school, and then support them in their jobs. Then I could spend much of my time with the students and faculty, be available and supportive of them—and try to solve problems fairly.

We had a student who was head of the Catholic Student Organization who did not fulfill his requirements to attend mandatory chapel. Instead of making him come back another year just to fulfill his chapel requirements as the academic dean asked, I thought of another way to work with the CSO to solve the problem. He still was not allowed to walk across the stage at commencement, but he was able to graduate. This was important, because the young man should not have been hampered in his college education by overly strict rules. That would not have been the entrepreneur's solution to this problem.

This same young man had come to me earlier and said the Catholic students needed more training in the Bible. I went to the priest at the Catholic church where I worshipped in a nearby town and asked him to come on Monday nights and have pizza with our kids while they were taught the Bible.

He said he did not feel confident doing that.

I then asked the bishop in Wichita to replace him with a young man who would teach our kids the Bible. The bishop made the change, and we had many satisfactory evenings talking about biblical matters.

By the summer of 2007, nearly two years after I had begun as president, the college still faced many challenges, but it was solvent, growing, and I was optimistic about its future. It was also the 120th anniversary of the college's founding by the Presbyterian Church as Cooper College. The name was changed to Sterling College in 1920.

I gave a speech to mark the occasion, in which I laid out the challenges facing the institution, and concluded:

"Come a little closer. Think about this. Get this picture in your mind. You've heard the premise, the problem, and now comes the payoff. Get a picture of a bright, elevated horizon for Sterling College in your mind. It's a view of an institution that is academically demanding and enthusiastically Christian, which we can realize together. We will not only survive, we will prevail. Your school is on its way to becoming the best institution of its kind in America."

When it came time to leave the following year, after three years of rebuilding the college, I wrote in the *Sterling Bulletin*:

"Dee and I leave with regret. My wife, the woman who didn't want to come to Kansas, now doesn't want to leave. She has made friends while participating in the town's wonderful activities and her life has been enhanced. I asked my lovely spouse if Schopenhauer said it properly when he proclaimed that young women choose their mates solely on the basis of their suitability as fathers.

"She said, 'Of course, and I would have married the other guy in ten minutes, but you had a plan and he did not.'

"I asked how she felt about the plan after 50 years.

"She replied, 'Actually it was a little more exciting and crazy than I anticipated.'

"I told Dee she'd made the best college president's wife I ever saw. She cared for students (at Sterling she established a clinic we didn't have, since she is a nurse), she was willing to accompany me raising money, and she entertained beautifully.

"I enjoyed the opportunity to make a difference in academe, however meager my talents, and am appreciative of the chance to serve. We will be leaving a part of us behind—and a part of our treasure. This great place has given us friends and insights that would not have come without the involvement of the people of the community and college family. Most importantly, perhaps, our faith has grown over this period. The two of us were devoted Christians on arrival, yet we now read our Bibles and pray together in a new way that demonstrates our enhanced commitment."

"My father was a schoolteacher, a socialist who eschewed making money. Pop believed the only way a person could be happy was to do for others. The college has allowed me to enhance the lives of young people, in some measure, and I am grateful. Schopenhauer also said, 'Knowledge requires talent and art requires genius,' and I make no claim to either. I expect no praise or approbation for the effort. I have received more than I have given.

In a Christian song entitled "Legacy," Nichole Nordeman speaks of recognition owed:

I don't mind if you've got something nice to say about me,
And I enjoy an accolade like the rest.
You could take my picture and hang it in a gallery
Of all who's who and so-n-so's that used to be the best
At such-n-such . . . it wouldn't matter much . . .

Not well traveled, not well read, not well-to-do or well bred,
Just want to hear instead, "Well done, good and faithful one."

"C'est ça.

Goodbye and thank you."

It was time to go home.

Leaving a team, structure, and wonderful assemblage of people in key roles at the college was difficult. Withdrawal wasn't hard, since I went back to work immediately, and needed to, since I had worked without salary at the college and contributed at least $100,000 per year to Sterling.

The man hired to replace me saw the situation differently. He got rid of my office, my house, my car, my assistant, and my academic dean. He also fired the school superintendent whom I had introduced to operations and community relations. In the process, Maurer removed a lot of the support structure he needed.

When I saw the vice presidents at an academic gathering in Atlanta eight months after Maurer had begun, they said, "He micromanages everything we do and requires us to report all of our activities. You set standards, gave us the right to pursue our goals, and supported us in everything we did."

When I returned to Sterling for a football game at the end of 2009, I asked my assistant to make appointments with Kansans who had been particularly important to me. One of them was Fran Jabara, an outstanding entrepreneur who had also been dean of the Wichita State Business School at an earlier time.

When I first met Fran in his office, he walked around the desk after about 30 minutes and said, "Every man needs a Lebanese friend. I would like to be your Lebanese friend."

The superintendent said he wanted to accompany me on a visit to Jabara, since he had not met him. During the meeting, Jabara asked me how the college was doing, and I said, "Fine."

On the way back from Wichita, Maurer said I did not like him or respect him because I had not described his tenure in glowing terms.

I replied that he was arrogant and ignorant, and that he should change his ways.

He did not and was fired about a year later.

When the interim president called me, he said the college's relationships with the town of Sterling were terrible. I replied that letting the superintendent go severed the tie to the town in significant ways. I had met with everyone he told me to see, had written a thousand words every week for the newspaper, and had gone down on Wednesday nights to see the publisher when he put the paper to bed. Small-town people do not support anyone who does not acknowledge them on a regular basis; that is, if you drive your car through town and do not wave at somebody, they are offended.

The Chairman of the Board of Trustees asked me to return but I declined. Dee, interestingly, would go back in a minute, for she enjoyed it there. She did well, meeting the people, starting a clinic at the school, going with me to raise money, and entertaining beautifully. I often told her she was the best president's wife I had ever met, and I meant it.

In academe, an entrepreneur with the proper focus and techniques can generate income, motivate people, build facilities, and attract students. This entails concern for people and their welfare, the ability to formulate and implant a vision, and an overwhelming desire to help others.

ALWAYS REMEMBER:

- There are four crucial aspects of academic administration: finances, faculty, facilities and freshman.

- Being a college president requires courage. Churchill called it grace under pressure. Socrates said that it required the ability to distinguish between real and perceived threats.

- Searching for meaning in an academic environment is crucial to guarantee its use for good. A historic Christian commitment to relationships and faith and reason is necessary to empower faculty and administrators.

- Working outside of your comfort zone gives you a chance to help people, taking risks and making a difference.

- The effective college president has to be entrepreneurial, taking risks and inspiring those around him with intelligence, compassion and charisma.

- Raising money for a college is not based on need, but in connecting donors to people and the prospects of success in academe.

- Success in the academic world means good students interacting with great faculty, professors who convince them to matriculate.

- Entrepreneurs live at right angles to the rest of the world, particularly in the academy.

- Politics, for a college, is difficult and demanding inside the walls and outside.

- A leader, in higher education, who is liked and respected will show progress and get things done. You will lead strong people with big egos who really care about students.

TEN

BE AN ENTREPRENEUR WITH YOUR WHOLE LIFE—NOT JUST YOUR BUSINESS

"Being on the tightrope is living; everything else is waiting."
—Karl Wallenda, high wire artist

"Excellence in the exercise of freedom is a virtue which
determines the worthiness of possession of goods. Happiness
is the total fulfillment of man's sensible nature."
—Immanuel Kant

"Be daring, be different, be impractical, be anything that will assert
integrity of purpose and imaginative vision against the play-it-safers,
the creatures of the common place, the slaves of the ordinary."
—Sir Cecil Beaton

I have always thought defining the word "entrepreneur" purely in a business sense was too limiting. I prefer to think of it in much broader terms: as a method of approaching everything. It is a choice to live on life's high wire, to enter situations that are precarious, challenging and potentially negative, and yet still be rubbing your hands and feeling delighted to be there.

Of course, you will not succeed every time. But then you roll on to the next deal, the next great opportunity, leaving any bad feelings behind. If you get mad at somebody and persist, they have control of you and your efforts, which they should not have. You do not want anyone to have that kind of influence over you. You do not want to give them that sort of weaponry to use on you. I have been treated badly by people and ignored, but I do not recriminate or respond particularly. You often have an opportunity to do that: to retaliate, to make somebody's life miserable. But it is easier to shrug things off.

Nothing beyond life and death is life and death.

To give myself the mental space to act and think like this, I have created certain disciplines in my life. I set aside time in each day, week, and month to daydream. There are certain physical places where I can get inspiration. We had this wonderful deck set up on Lake Erie, and I would sit there on a Saturday morning and everything would become clear for me. Thus comes insight.

I keep coming back to the same books, those that have influenced me most deeply, such as Dale Carnegie's *How to Win Friends and Influence People*. Dee will say, "I am going to give Dale Carnegie to somebody," and I say, "I'd like to read it again first."

I have a notebook that has various categories, information on the boards I am on and my 100 personal credos. (An example: **If**

someone lies to you once, they will lie to you forever.) I look at it every week. For my company there is a budget, a list of licenses, a summary of work items to accomplish, tax considerations, and the like. On the personal side, there are items that must be done this year, including painting (painting occupies the mind and liberates the spirit better than golf), education outreach, brand extension, personal/professional connections to be made (restaurateurs, head-hunters, public relations people, politicians, journalists, and so on), self-development courses needed, dollar targets for net worth and debt, image considerations, and relationships (18 people with whom I deal with through contact, small personal favors, and delivering value—I send a bottle of wine with a note bimonthly since I am not in continuous contact).

On each strategic point, I have a list of tactics to follow through the year. I have a weekly cash position for personal and company dollars, a summary of investments, which allows me to evaluate firms buying stocks and bonds. There is a list of items I must do to be the person I wish to become in 12 months, such as replacement of bad habits, expansion of the brand, organizations to join or quit. I also have a list of good items: association with bright and important people, elegance, technical challenge, growth, social standing, health, croquet, development impact, and the like. There is also a list of people I wish to emulate, people whose skills and successes are exemplary: Roger Penske, John Block (publisher of the *Toledo Blade* newspaper), John Silber, Dick Anderson (Toledo's leading civic con-tributor), Jim Seneff, Richard Branson, Frank Lloyd Wright, Dwight Eisenhower, and Ralph Lauren. There is a compilation of areas that should be avoided, as well: Toledo politics, retired people, inveterate golfers, debt, other women, excessive risk, and idleness.

If this sounds like micromanagement, then perhaps it is. But it is my way of ensuring that no day goes wasted. It is to help me stay up there on the high wire. As I have watched my friends and peers become more cautious over time, I have seen my own personal risks diminishing. I have made all the money I could ever need, and my children are independent. If everything went to smash, I feel I could start over and do it again, which is one of the wonderful things about America.

One of the most important pieces of advice I have ever received was to "expose yourself to others."

This means express your thoughts, hopes, and fears to other people as a means of making progress and building relationships. Do not pretend to be anything but what you are. Try what you want to try, say what is in your heart, because that is how you will discover the deepest echoes in those around you.

> **RESPONSIBILITIES OF AN ENTREPRENEUR:**
> As an entrepreneur, you have a responsibility to make the world a better place. You have certain God-given and rare talents that must be applied for the benefit of others. Do your best to help. That means giving money and time. You have to do the work. If you do, and you are engaged in the process, then you can make a difference and you can be the person others turn to.

As I said at the start of this book, one of the greatest satisfactions of being an entrepreneur is becoming a person to whom people turn to get things done. You give people such a clear sense of who you are and what you are capable of that they come to you the way they would to a favorite restaurant or shop.

They need to remember the direction to you. They say, "Oh, for that, we need to go to Bruce."

When I was in construction, I always hated groundbreakings, those phony ceremonies when the local politicians would meet the developers, and they all put on hard hats and pretend they are shoveling dirt. What I loved were dedications, because you could celebrate completion and what you had done. Similarly, at college, I loved commencements, because they spoke of both achievement and possibility.

The best lives are full of excitement and variety, of freshness and difficulty, and that sense of vertigo that comes from putting yourself in a position up there on the wire, with the spotlight on you, where you might fall.

That is the way an entrepreneur has to live, and it brings the richest rewards.

I have given a number of commencement speeches. Once, while preparing to speak at the Rollins College graduation exercises, I was in Saratoga Springs at a Democratic Party enclave with Mario Cuomo. When I mentioned I was giving a commencement speech, Cuomo asked me how long it was, and I said "Twenty minutes."

Cuomo said that was much too long, that the proper address was only eight minutes, with four parts—showing you belong there as someone in academe, identifying your skills, giving a message, and having a great conclusion. He said if I would send my speech to one of his people, she would help me with it, and she did.

When I was walking out to the podium with the president of Rollins College, Rita Bornstein, I told that story and she said, "Start your speech that way."

I did and it was probably the high point of the address. It started with "Mothers, fathers, grandparents, children, friends, faculty, honored guests, and others, there they are, the class of 1984. You never thought they'd make it, did you?"

The next speech I give will start with an admonition not to wear seat belts, since this gives government control in your life that you do not want. As this is written, I have just gotten two seat belt infraction tickets, each worth $140. Obviously others do not have the faith in air bags that I do.

Cuomo was speaking at Stanford soon after we met, and I asked my daughter, who attended that school and was a junior, to go to commencement and listen to him. She said he spoke eight minutes, was able in all the categories, and was impressive.

No one remembers a commencement speaker, typically, but I remember hers in 1984. They had asked Gorbachev but could not clear him into that sensitive area of the country, had rejected Bill Cosby because he wanted $50,000 and an honorary degree, and settled on Ted Koppel.

Koppel stood up and said, "President [Donald] Kennedy, etc., if you are waiting for Gorbachev or Cosby, I suggest you stop thinking about them. I am your commencement speaker." He had them in the palm of his hand.

Let's look at Niccolò Machiavelli, who lived from 1469 to 1527, and whose philosophy still echoes today. He was an administrator and a diplomat in the Florentine Republic and traveled to France and Germany. He knew political leaders throughout the countries of his travels—most significantly Cesare Borgia, presumably the model for the title character in *The Prince*. Machiavelli was accused of complicity, imprisoned, and tortured. He was left without position, though later exonerated, and retired to a meager farm near San Casciano. In this bucolic setting, in near poverty, his days filled with prosaic discourse with the local peasantry, he wrote *The Prince* and the *Discourses*, determined to prove that banishment had made him neither idle nor ineffective. He addressed *The Prince* to Lorenzo d'Medici, as the ruler who would return Florence to its former glory. The city states of Renascence Italy had fallen into a morass of inept rulers and foreign domination. The traits that Machiavelli espoused were clemency, faithfulness, frankness, humanity, religion, greatness, boldness, gravity, and strength. One should eschew being fickle, frivolous, effeminate, cowardly, and irresolute. Machiavelli said entrepreneurs were simply those who understood there was little difference between obstacle and opportunity and were able to turn both to their advantage.

One entrepreneur has said, "Generally, the worse the circumstances, the better I like it. I know it can improve the situation and people are much more willing to let me take strong steps when things are going bad."

An entrepreneur's identity is a mild form of mania; success is possible in various spheres. It can transform your life and the lives of those around you if you drive for innovation, pursue "crazy" ideas, reject a reasonable idea that will lead to defeat, find purpose and satisfaction in chaotic situations, and use your enthusiasm for life as a means to success. **It helps tremendously if you are positive, kind, humble, compassionate, grateful, patient, and selfless.**

You must decide what is important to you as you pursue your goals. For me, that encompasses:

- family values,
- the highest ethical standards,

- the treatment of others with respect, dignity, and concern,
- the use of energy as your most precious resource,
- working with high physical, mental, and emotional fitness, and
- the desire to make a lasting difference.

You must bring passion and positive energy along with hope to face life's challenges. You must never surrender your spirit. You must realize you can analyze all that is possible, but then must trust your instincts and your faith in God. The Almighty has a plan for you, and it will be presented to you, usually when you least expect it.

Great managers break all the rules of conventional wisdom, for they believe, as Wallenda said, that being on the tightrope is the only way to live. **Entrepreneurs know you will never succeed unless you risk failure.**

It is a risk to go from being a businessman to being a politician. There are attributes that help. I could manage the fundraising and the expenditure part of it because of my business experience. Finding other supportive people was a learned skill, built on compassion and concern for the individuals. You can involve them in a mission which, remember, J. S. Mill described as anticipating an idea that will become acceptable to future generations.

As a political candidate, my speaking skills were deficient. They gave me speeches to memorize and read, but they did not work. In two weeks I learned it was only necessary to stand up and speak from your heart about the concerns of the people of the state of Ohio, the need for change, and the opportunities for the future.

Translating those skills into an academic environment was a challenge. Understanding the numbers was important, fundraising was crucial, and building a team was the same as it was in business. Faculty support is difficult to come by, though. My habit of walking around the campus and dropping into professors' offices, unannounced, to talk about their plans and the needs of their disciplines helped me engender this crucial support from my staff.

A college president I know well has just experienced a vote of "no confidence" from his faculty. The action is a result, almost entirely, of this man not interacting with the professors in that way. They find him elusive, unconcerned, and arrogant. He is, however, a capable administrator, a man with foresight about the future of higher education, and a fine scientist.

When Paul O'Neill took over Alcoa, he stated that his number one purpose was safety. By emphasizing safety, he showed people he cared about their lives and their livelihood. The results were dramatic in the expansion of the company and the growth of its earnings.

People must see, understand, and identify with your
vision of the future.

That takes repetitive action, which an entrepreneur does not welcome, but it is essential. Like effective scientists, they see an outcome, embrace it, and then seek to prove they have the right result.

THE ENTREPRENEURIAL PERSONALITY:

There is an eccentricity of personality that ties innovative people together. The big five personality factors are extroversion, agreeableness, conscientiousness, neuroticism, and openness to experience and ideas. Most entrepreneurs' personalities tend to extroversion; if they are to succeed, they must be open to new ideas and approaches.

There is statistically significant inheritability associated with all of the big five personality factors, including openness to new experiences and ideas. Many people are happy to tell you something is impossible or too risky. You have to be a person who is willing to discard all of that, which really makes no sense. It is kind of a fearlessness or irrationality. This gets the same people into trouble but leads to really outstanding innovations.

Consider the movie *October Sky*. It is about a guy who grew up in a little coal mining town around the time of Sputnik in the late 1950s and early 1960s. He fell in love with the idea of building rockets. The movie follows him through his high school years, and he ends up becoming an engineer at NASA. It is inspirational, and I always come out of that movie wanting to work harder.

Remember, George Bernard Shaw stated that all progress depends on the unreasonable man. This individual must find his voice and inspire others to find theirs. He or she must think win-win in professional and personal pursuits. That individual must, in the latter case, be appreciative and grateful for family, affluence, intelligence, and physical well-being. With courage, intelligence, and compassion, a fruitful life can emerge from a genetically-based mild form of mania, which has endowed the entrepreneur with unusual energy, creativity, enthusiasm, and a propensity for taking on challenges. Challenges can be met in many fields when those traits are manifest.

A hypomanic personality, coupled with acculturation early in life that anything is possible, means you must experience and express what is in your genes. You say to yourself, continuously, "That is a difficult challenge, but I can meet it."

Never believe that one person, one small decision, cannot create dramatic change. I remember when they confiscated the vegetable cart of a 26-year-old Tunisian named Mohamed Bouazizi, which meant he could no longer support his family of eight. The city refused to help him. Bouazizi set himself on fire in protest. The people of Tunisia took up Bouazizi's cause, and in less than a month, replaced Tunisia's government.

In this hypomanic way of life, you learn a lot about yourself. Perhaps that is one of the most important motivating factors. Your belief system is that you can meet the challenge you seek, and you have to learn what that entails. You test yourself continuously against your psychological makeup and belief system. That testing is crucial.

When I was picked up at the Wichita airport by one of Sterling College's administrators to take the job as president there, I remember thinking on the 60-mile ride to the school that I was all alone, one man seeking to make change and make progress against odds. In that case, you have to say to yourself that you have the skills to do the job. You want to manifest those skills for the benefit of others and to satisfy your personal creed. When things are going poorly you have to depend on those beliefs. When matters turn around and there is progress, you experience a great deal of satisfaction, directly and vicariously, from the events proceeding well.

You take these risks, believing you can do it based on your heredity and experience. The experience—putting yourself forward in difficult situations—leads to understanding yourself and the cosmos around you. Somewhere, those synapses were connected in a way that makes you believe the risk is not only worth taking but also worth surmounting, fulfilling. What is in the back of a hypomanic entrepreneur's head, however difficult it is to reach, is that there is an answer to that question that others cannot find and it is worth the travail to unearth a solution.

Failure is not an option. When you ask the great mountain climbers why they would attempt to scale a peak that has not been climbed before, some might say, "Because it's there." That, to me, says they believe they are wired to do something that another cannot. They cannot fail to take the challenge. A study by Cooper, Woo, and Dunkelberg in 1988 of almost 3,000 entrepreneurs revealed that fully one-third of them believed their chances of success were 100 percent, though in reality about 75 percent of new businesses fail within five years. Obviously, in your life, others can do what you cannot. Yet there are situations where you say to yourself, "Why not me? I can solve this."

Like soldiers in the battle zone who fervently believe it is the other guy who will be killed, new entrepreneurs typically believe others may fall along the wayside, but they will not. When I was in the Navy, my neighbor was a military pilot who was lost at night over the Pacific. When a plane went down and a colleague was killed, as this man was, we would go to the officer's club, drink a lot, and sing songs like "Perils of the Air." Each pilot would say it could not possibly happen to him. Without that belief, the pilot probably would not have gone up the next day. The wives attended these events, and you could see they believed it could occur tomorrow, that any one of them could die.

Uniquely determined personality traits of entrepreneurs are openness to new experiences, receptivity to change, and willingness to assume risks—these are genetically based, inheritable. A couple of relevant examples might be illustrative.

Dana Corporation, a $2 billion dollar enterprise in Toledo, Ohio, was transformed by a man named Ren McPherson. He believed all authority should be pushed as far down an organization as possible. On his watch, he reduced the company code of regulations from four huge binders to two pages. He also held that in a nine-foot-square space around the machine in one of his factories, the operator of the equipment knew more about his business than he, Ren, did. He spent a good deal of time on the factory floor, talking to people, learning, and motivating them. He called together his key executives in interactive sessions called "Hell Weeks," where he challenged individuals and encouraged responses to the problems at hand. Probably Ren took these actions not only for motivational reasons but because he enjoyed the exercise, that search for change. He certainly created a different corporation in the process.

Then there is the story of the scorpion that goes to a dog and asks to be transported on the other animal's back across the river.

The dog says, "No, when we're in the middle of the river, you'll bite me and I'll drown."

The scorpion responds, "That's ridiculous, if I did that, I'd drown, too!"

Recognizing that logic, the dog has the scorpion jump on his back and starts to cross the river. Partway across, the scorpion reaches down and bites him on the shoulder.

The dog says, "Now we'll both die, why did you do that?"

The scorpion's answer: "That's just the way I am."

That may be illustrative of the entrepreneur.

To apply these skills with that special belief is a driving force. That force, it seems to me, pervades business, politics, academe, public service, and challenges in other arenas. There is a commonality of skills necessary for accomplishment. I once had dinner with Peter Grace, who left Yale at age 19 to run the family business, the W. R. Grace Company, a NYSE firm. I asked him why he was successful.

He said, "I'm good at the numbers."

He was also good with people, analytical thought, technology, organization, and politics. Most importantly, Peter was built and trained from birth to believe he could make a difference.

A person with a hypomanic personality takes risks because of the way his brain is formed. There are no outer limits to this individual's sense of what can be accomplished. From Sam Calgione: "There is a sometimes rapturous feeling accompanied with entrepreneurial activities, someone witnesses a vision come true and sees the reflection of that vision in the eyes of customers and coworkers while participating in a development of magical, culturally transforming entity. This is a surge of hormones at such times, behavioral genetics research tells us."

Feynman called it "the kick of discovery," the pleasure of finding things out.

There is a Rotter Scale that measures an individual's locus of internal control; that is the extent to which a person believes they determine their own success and control their own performance. Evans and Leighton found that individuals with high Rotter Score values—reflecting a belief that they control their own destinies—were more likely to become entrepreneurs and start their own businesses.

A person with this type of personality has been responsible for the major progress in the government, the military, the church, and other institutions, evoking change to enable progress. Nature does not pervade all of the members of a particular family. The hypomanic differs. You can teach entrepreneurship to a transactional personality type, but it is the opposite of how they think, and it is difficult.

This drives Phillip Kotler, a marketing professor at Northwestern University, to use the "science" side of marketing for art museums, blood banks, Friends of the Earth, and cities, involving a holistic concept characterized by relationship marketing, internal marketing, integrated and socially responsive marketing.

Thus the entrepreneur can function in various areas and disciplines, motivated by the kick that Feynman describes, the thrill of accomplishment, the challenge of problem solving and growth, and the hypomanic need to excel. What he will not be is described in this little poem:

A centipede was happy quite, until a toad in the fun

Said, "Pray which leg comes after which?"

This raised his doubts to such a pitch he fell distracted in the ditch

Not knowing how to run.

- The Distracted Centipede —Anonymous

DOUBT THE EXPERTS

Richard Feynman said we learn from science that you must doubt the experts. Science is the belief in the ignorance of the experts. This thought drives entrepreneurs forward. One of Feynman's lessons for entrepreneurs is that if you start working on a problem, you must look around every once in a while and find out if the original motives are still right, as he did not do when the war with Germany was over and they kept developing the bomb.

The constitutional condition, and its acculturation, allows an entrepreneur to be effective in various arenas. Richard Branson has excelled with music, airlines, vodka, cola, cosmetics, and now the Virgin Green Fund to grow the renewable energy and resource efficiency sectors—all of this after leaving school at age 17 to start a magazine called *Student*.

An entrepreneur, as the unreasonable man, has the opportunity to break the rules, live on the high wire, accept unreasonable challenge with a sure feeling of success, earn happiness through achievement, and make progress. Most significantly, all these factors can work for the individual in multiple venues. In business, politics, academe, and public service, the skills that drive the hypomanic individual can be effective.

Entrepreneurship has the power to do much more than just create successful businesses; it can transform the world. As an entrepreneur, you have that power. Apply the concepts in this book to your own daily life and you, too, can become *An Entrepreneur for ALL Seasons*.

ALWAYS REMEMBER:

- Be a person who will assert integrity of purpose and imaginative vision against the conservative creatures of the ordinary place.

- Apply your God-given talents for the benefit of others.

- Inheriting a hypomanic personality requires you to experience and express what is in your genes.

- A little caution avoids great regrets; hope for the best and prepare for the worst.

- Success comes quickly to those who develop great powers of intense sustained concentration.

- Enthusiasm covers many deficiencies and will make others want to associate with you.

- All human beings are driven by two basic emotions – pain and pleasure. Most people will do far more to avoid pain than they will to gain pleasure.

- Do not compromise when you are right. Hold your ground, show no fear and ask for what you want.

- If the situation is not right in the long term, walk away from it for you need a long term outlook in all your endeavors.

- Out think, out innovate and out hustle the competition, and vividly visualize yourself as winning before entering into every deal or competitive situation.

- First impressions are lasting impressions; put your best foot forward.

- People treat you like you teach them to treat you.

- A success key is to position yourself at the top of others' agenda.

- Producing results is more important than proving you're right.

- Understand others frames of references, points of views, needs and wants to determine what is honest, fair, effective and rational; then act accordingly.

- Enjoy life, it's an adventure. You can care passionately about the outcome, but keep it in perspective.

- Be responsible for who, what, and where you are in life. Situations aren't important; how you react to them is.

- Geniuses delegate the 90% of work that they're not best at, and spend all their time on their unique ability.

- Patience is profitable. Achievement comes from the sum of consistent small efforts, repeated daily.

- Question everything; don't believe it's true or right just because it's conventional.

- The surest way to accomplish your business goals is by making service to others your primary goal.

- Lasting success comes from within yourself by producing values not by consuming them.

- The best investment you will ever make is your steady increase of knowledge.

- Anxiety is usually caused by lack of control, organization, preparation and action.

Salary and Level I Want/Need

	LEVEL	SALARY
MAX		10,000,000
	REWARDS	
MIN		1,000,000

A chance to exercise creative leadership with intellectual stimulation, using my expertise, helping others gaining rapport, influence, power & fame.

Kinds of PEOPLE I Like to Use These Skills With

Men in a group of eight or less, of my age, social background & wealth who are easy to work with.

Both sexes, of all ages, with like social & economic skills who are easy to work with.

Tools or Means: 1

Kinds of INFORMATION I Like to Use These Skills With

FORM	CONTENT
1. Books	1. Programs
2. Magazines	2. Principles
3. Newspapers	3. Systems
4. Goals	4. Goals
5. Ideas	5. New Approaches
6. Concept Loss	6. Performance
7. Surveys	Characteristics

Tools or Means: 2

Kinds of THINGS I Like to Use These Skills With

1. Paper
2. Machines
3. Cards
4. Money
5. Books, magazines & newspapers
6. Oceans
7. Balloons
8. Automobiles

Tools or Means: 3

The Physical Setting I Like to Work In

1. Important & Interesting work
2. Good business climate
3. Control
4. Respect
5. Good "earnings"
6. Bright, tractable people
7. Risk avoidance
8. Stylish & Professional environment
9. Technical involvement

Spiritual or Emotional Setting I Like to Work In

1. My life must have a meaning and contribute to others. Must use my technical and leadership skills for better world.
2. Must support family.
3. Must live with wealth, style and grace.
4. Must be right with God, receiving his blessing and guidance.
5. Must own projects people respect.
6. Must associate with bright people.
7. Must have special home, car, sunlight, access to water.

What I Like to Do with TASKS

1. Leading, taking the lead being a pioneer
2. Initiating, starting up, founding or establishing
3. Persuading, motivating, recruiting or selling
4. Problem solving, or seeing patterns from a mass of data
5. Planning, laying out a step-by-step process for attaining a goal
6. Following through, getting things done, producing
7. Communicating well in conversation or in writing
8. Guiding a group discussion, communicating warmth, to reach goal

Outcomes

Be in command, develop and build, organize and operating/shaping and influencing and gaining recognition.

Make a difference, an impact in an important way for society by building a new installation/service organization and being recognized for such.

TRANSFORM YOUR LIFE AND THE LIVES OF THOSE AROUND YOU

D r. Bruce Douglas has used his business acumen and entrepreneurial talent in all facets of life. From business and academe to politics and civic endeavors, Bruce has used entrepreneurship to achieve success with his endeavors in each of these arenas. Now, with An Entrepreneur is for ALL Seasons, Bruce shares how others can use their skills and talents to impact those around them, get things done and truly make a positive difference in the world.

Let Bruce's experiences and advice inspire you as an entrepreneur and leader to take your skills and success to new heights. Bruce is available for plenary sessions, conference keynotes, leadership roundtables, academic commencements, panel discussions, and more. His programs can be customized to meet your organization's unique goals and objectives.

For more information about bringing Bruce to your organization or next event, visit DrBruceDouglas.com.

Printed in the USA
CPSIA information can be obtained
at www.ICGtesting.com
JSHW012027140824
68134JS00033B/2922